Coloring Book of Shadows

Planner for A Magical

2022

Amy Cesari

Are You Afraid to Start Coloring?!

Take this free magical art class and get started with your colored pencils:

COLORINGBOOKOFSHADOWS.COM/COLORING-COURSES/

Print and color free pages. Get them at:

ColoringBookOfShadows.com

Fire Safety Disclaimer:

(Hazardous & Unsafe Witchcraft)　　　　(Fire-Safe Witchcraft)

The images in this book are for decorative purposes—they are not realistic guides for arranging flame-based altars. Always place a fireproof dish beneath candles & incense. Leave clearance above & around flames. Do not place flammable objects near flames and never leave flaming things or incense unattended. Readers of this book take full responsibility when using fire.

> > > > > Fill out your birth chart on the next page. You'll find instructions and explanations in the introduction of this book.

JANUARY
SATURN
WHAT'S MOST IMPORTANT?

FEBRUARY
URANUS
WHAT'S MY UNIQUE MAGIC?

MARCH
NEPTUNE
WHAT IS MY DREAM?

APRIL
MARS
WHAT MUST I DO?

MAY
VENUS
WHAT DO I DESIRE?

JUNE
MERCURY
WHAT DO I NEED TO KNOW?

JULY
MOON
WHAT DO I FEEL?

Pull tarot cards, cast rune stones, or write your own words of wisdom for each month of the year. Fill them all out at the beginning of the year, or do it month-by month as a "look ahead" or a reflection of what's passed.

SEPTEMBER
MERCURY
HOW CAN I BE RESPONSIBLE?

OCTOBER
VENUS
HOW CAN I BALANCE?

DECEMBER
JUPITER
HOW CAN I GROW?

NOVEMBER
PLUTO
WHAT DO I NOT KNOW?

AUGUST
THE SUN
WHO DO I WANT TO BE?

About this Book

To make your year magical, all you really have to do is get to know yourself better.

The most widely accepted definition of magic is that magic is the ability to influence your destiny. To harness intention, will, and the natural forces already in play, such as the moon, the sun, the planets, and the changing seasons, also known as the Wheel of the Year.

And knowing yourself is a crucial step in working with magic. You exist in a world of endless possibilities. When you know yourself, you can stay "in your power" and direct that power towards what you desire, no matter what is going on around you.

Astrology is a mystical art of self-discovery. While ancient astrologers believed that planetary alignments affected the Earth energetically, one of the more modern interpretations is that the cosmos are like a mirror—As Above, So Below.

We see ourselves in the archetypes, myths, stories, and structure of the planets and stars. And the exploration of these archetypes will ask you the question of who you are. So... who are you?! How will you answer?

It takes courage to be yourself, to do magic, and to see what happens when you set an intention or cast a spell. But when you follow your soul's calling—no matter the surrounding circumstances—you'll find your power.

You are made of stars, and you have the magic of the cosmos in the palm of your hand.

Try it! Put your hands out, close your eyes, and feel a ball of light or energy build.

You already have what you need to make the most of your magical life. All you have to do is start. Are you ready? Say "Yes!"

Tips to Use This Planner

• Please don't stress about "keeping up" on coloring the whole book. You can color none of it, some of it, or all of it. Enjoy the parts you do, and don't worry if it doesn't get "done."

• Since this book is printed on both sides of the paper, it works best if you use colored pencils, crayons, or ballpoint pens. Markers will bleed through to the other side.

• Write, color, and draw in this book! Take notes. Expressing your thoughts in writing is a powerful way to create your reality. Here are some ideas of what to write:

- Your day-to-day-mundane appointments
- A daily gratitude journal
- Daily reflections
- Daily tarot
- A diary of your spiritual journey
- Messages from your intuition

• "Spellcasting Basics" are included to show you how to cast a circle, ground and center, and perform a "full" spell. If you are new to spells, please be sure to read this.

• Always remember, the magic is inside you! Even if you start this book "late" in the year, or if it isn't "the best" moon phase, you are the most powerful force in your own life. The seasons, sun, and moon are only tools to help you unlock the magic you already have.

Goals, Plans, and Intentions

Yes, this is a planner, but that doesn't mean you have to get intense about... planning. It's about getting to know what you *really* want first and then using the powers of the universe to give you a boost. Work witchier, not harder! Here are some tips:

- Less is more. Go for broader feelings and intentions rather than super specific dates, processes, and outcomes. Leave room for magic to surprise you in fantastic ways.
- Make your goals as big or as small as you want. Your goal or plan could be to do less.
- Instead of saying what you don't want, "to stop being an emotional wreck," phrase it positively so you feel good when you say it, "to feel at ease with my emotions."
- Any plans you make are more of a guideline. Don't be afraid to scrap them and do something else if they don't feel right anymore. It's never too late to change directions or make new plans—in fact, that's often where the best magic comes in.

Using Your Intuition

So how do you use your intuition? Follow your emotions. Emotions and intuition are woven of the same thread. Even if (especially if) you've been called "too emotional," you can trust your emotions to be your guide. If something makes you feel "icky"— hurt, bad, anxious, nervous, hurried, chained, or dreary—stop and listen. Then figure out the message, work through it, let go of the unpleasant feelings, and restore your emotional balance by steering yourself to what feels better. Ask yourself, "Is this what I feel I *should* be doing, instead of what feels right for me?" And, "Is this what I want to do, or what someone else wants me to do?"

Can it really be that simple? Yes. It's the key to get you going in the right direction that only YOU can feel at any moment. So... which direction is that, exactly? The one that makes you feel happier, excited, hopeful, or curious. The one that feels better. Go that way.

Dark, Light, and Shadow Selves

Following your good-feeling intuition doesn't mean you're "ignoring" your dark side. Just as the year has a dark half, we've all got a dark side or shadow selves—many of them. They are the unseen and often ignored parts of ourselves—self-doubt, low self-esteem, jealousy, fear of what we truly desire, unworthiness, unhealthy habits, and stuckness.

Whether you see shadows as obscuring the light or light as creating the shadows, this balance offers you powerful clues to understand and explore your purpose.

So... know that darkness. Use it. Acknowledge it. Know that both light and dark are essential halves of the magical seasons of your life, and the work is to walk through the shadows in order to transcend to a place of spiritual balance, purpose, and fulfillment. And, yes, this is a super-deep topic. There is so much more to explore here, so be sure to follow it if it calls you!

ASTROLOGY
The Big Picture

*Not quite to scale!
(& UNFATHOMABLY BIGGER)

Astrology is thousands of years old and practiced across many cultures. This book focuses on "Western" astrology.

Astrology is an observation and analysis of the positions of the planets, Earth's moon, and sun in our solar system and how they travel around the starry backdrop of the sky.

Ancient astrologers used twelve constellations of stars as visual reference points, known as the zodiac signs. These constellations appear to move around Earth like a wheel.

Astrologers also divided the sky into twelve "fixed" reference points like pie slices—the houses. The houses are calculated depending on the viewer's time and location on Earth.

Our solar system is at the "center" of the zodiac wheel. As the sun, Earth's moon, and the planets travel "through" the zodiac signs

You Are Here
*APPROXIMATELY

HELLO STARSHINE

and houses, their alignments influence or mirror what happens on Earth.

It might help to visualize the zodiac as a swirling ring of constellations around our solar system. If you've struggled with the "big picture" of astrology, try using a free "star finder" app on your phone or tablet. *Sky View* and *Night Sky* are two excellent free choices, but there are many others.

Spend a few minutes on a clear night looking at the constellations, the moon, the planets, and their positions across the zodiac, both with your unaided eyes and through the reference of the app.

These apps can be a game-changer to see, feel, and understand the positions of the zodiac and the planets in the sky above you.

PLANETS, SIGNS, & HOUSES

When you're first exploring astrology, it's easy to get confused with the interplay of planets, zodiac signs, and houses.

• **Planets represent "what" you do or what you desire.** These are the big motivational energies of the solar system. The term "planets" includes the sun and moon. The planets are like archetypal stories or quests that represent the trials we face along the human journey.

• **Signs show "how" you interact and react on planetary quests.** Signs are like parts of your personality that emerge as you go through the journey of life.

• **Houses show "where" all of this is likely to go down.** Houses represent different facets of your day-to-day life and can show you where to look for clues to personal growth and fulfillment.

PLANETS - "WHAT YOU DO"

Planets are the forces of motivational energy that can influence what you do or what you desire. Planets drive us.

It's important to note that classical astrology includes our sun and moon under the label of "planets."

Ancient people believed the planets represented the will of the gods. Most modern interpretations view the planets more like archetypal myths. Planets are the trials, tribulations, and quests of life.

Our sun, for example, is the "planet" that represents the motivations and desires of your self expression. Mercury represents desires of your mind. Venus, your love. Mars, your power. The moon, your emotions, and so on (more later).

SIGNS - "HOW YOU DO IT"

The twelve zodiac signs show "how" you express "what" you do. The signs are like traits of your personality or your ways of operating in life.

For example, the moon sign of your birth chart shows "how" the moon (the planet of emotion) influences you or how you do emotional things.

If your moon sign is Libra, you will often express your emotional desires (the "what" of the moon) through finding balance (the "how" of Libra). And if your moon is Aries, you'll be apt to express emotional desires (the "what" of the moon) quickly and honestly (the "how" of Aries)—meaning you won't be afraid to speak your mind when emotions are high.

HOUSES - "WHERE YOU DO IT"

The houses show "where" these energies are likely to emerge in daily life.

Things like money, friendships, spirituality, your home, health, and environment—these houses are areas of life where your motivations (planets) and personality (signs) interact and entwine with the world around you.

Going back to the previous example, the moon in Aries, if it's in your 5th house of creativity, you'll have a tendency to speak your mind when you pursue your art.

If your moon in Aries falls in the 7th house on your birth chart, you'll likely find yourself speaking up in emotional situations when you are dealing with partnerships and relationships.

And if the moon is currently in Aries, *everyone* will have an influence of speaking up in emotional situations—even if they do not have the moon in Aries in their birth chart.

PLANETARY POWERS

Planets are the forces of motivational energy that can influence what you do or what you desire. And remember, classical astrology calls our sun and moon "planets" as well.

Ancient people believed the planets represented the will of the gods. Most modern interpretations view the planets more like archetypal myths. The planets represent the stories of life that we all experience. And the locations of the planets in the houses and zodiac signs of your birth chart are what make your stories unique.

THE SUN, MOON, AND INNER PLANETS:

This group of "inner" planets and luminaries relate to personal characteristics of who you are and what you're motivated to do.

THE SUN wields immense power. Without it, life on Earth (as we know it) would not exist.

When someone asks, "What's your sign?" it usually refers to the zodiac sign of the sun at the time of your birth. The sun represents outward self-expression and your sense of purpose and creativity. It begins to answer the question, "Who am I?" — but it's only one part of the picture.

The sun completes its transit through the entire zodiac in 365 days—a calendar year on Earth—and stays in each sign for one month.

THE MOON represents your emotional and subconscious motivations or desires. Often hidden, but willing to reveal themselves in time—you'll find the emotions of the moon in the subconscious—the depths of your soul. Your moon sign represents who you are on the inside when you are not fully aware of it—the other side of how you express yourself outwardly (the sun).

The moon takes 28 days to orbit the Earth, passing through each zodiac sign for about two-and-a-half days.

MERCURY is the planet of the mind and drives communication, mental outlook, and cognitive processes like reading, writing, and analyzing. Mercury will guide you on quests of knowledge and information gathering.

The closest planet to the sun, Mercury orbits in just 88 Earth days. From our perspective on Earth, Mercury stays in each zodiac sign for a range of fifteen to sixty Earth days, with infamous periods of retrograde (more on this later!).

VENUS is the planet of romance, pleasure, love, beauty, and comfort. Venus will fuel your desires for harmonious surroundings (like pillows and blankets!) and that sumptuous feeling of love.

Venus completes its orbit in 225 Earth days and stays in each sign for one to two months.

MARS is about action and drive. This planet signifies your desire to do things and shows what motivates you to be courageous and brave. Mars will lead the way for you to take bold action.

Mars orbits the sun and completes a zodiac cycle in about 2 Earth years—staying in each zodiac sign for approximately a month and a half.

THE SUN   THE MOON   MERCURY   VENUS   MARS

THE OUTER PLANETS:

The "giant" planets, Jupiter and Saturn, drive your interactions with others. Unlike the inner planets, guides of inner quests, these "social" planets influence how you interact with society and culture.

JUPITER represents education, philosophy, and expansion of all things including money and material possessions, as well as achievements and opportunities. Jupiter is extremely large. It will propel you on your quest to find out how your beliefs and views help society evolve on a broader scale. Jupiter takes about twelve Earth years to orbit the sun and spends one year in each sign.

SATURN is about contraction, the opposite of Jupiter's expansion. Saturn represents a focused reduction of excess and a return to what is essential in life.

Saturn is about responsibility and how much (or how little!) you are compelled to follow the rules. Saturn will challenge you with structure, limitations, timekeeping, and self-discipline.

Saturn takes about thirty years to orbit the sun and will stay in each sign for two-and-a-half years.

THE OUTER-OUTER PLANETS: These farthest transpersonal planets are about our journeys through the world of the spiritual—of dreams, intuition, and the unknown.

URANUS: "Well, I never saw THAT coming." Thrown off guard or delightfully surprised by something unexpected?! That's Uranus. Uranus is the twist in the story, the true WTF moments in life that make you laugh, cry, or both.

Uranus is the planet of invention, revolution, radical change, unabashed originality, freedom, liberation from societal norms, and moments in life that feel like "breakthrough" discoveries.

Uranus stays in each zodiac sign for about seven Earth years, and it takes eighty-four years to complete its cycle around the sun and zodiac.

NEPTUNE is the planet of dreams and of the unknown. It leads you on quests of mysticism, spirituality, exploring ideas, and intuition.

If you've felt an inner calling to become a witch or forest-dwelling oracle—that's Neptune.

Neptune is quite languid and slow. It stays in each sign for about fourteen Earth years with long periods of retrograde. Neptune completes a zodiac and sun cycle in 164 Earth years.

PLUTO was discovered in 1930 and is a modern addition to astrology. It is the ruler of the underworld and the planet that may take you on the quest of deep spiritual transformation.

Pluto represents the powers of creation and destruction and the necessity of metaphorical "death" in order to transform. Because of its long transits between signs, Pluto represents the journey of the soul's awakening.

Pluto stays in each sign for twelve to thirty-one Earth years, so you'll only experience a handful of Pluto transits in your life. It takes Pluto 248 Earth years to complete a zodiac cycle.

AND MORE: There are some fascinating, esoteric points that were left out due to space considerations. Research Nodes, Chiron, Lilith, and more if they call to you.

JUPITER   SATURN   URANUS   NEPTUNE   PLUTO

12 ZODIAC SIGNS

The planets are the driving forces of "what" we do and the quests we go on, and the zodiac signs are parts of our personalities and behaviors that show "how" we interact with the world.

Although each zodiac sign has a planetary "ruler," each planet travels through all the signs. Think of the "planetary ruler" as the CEO of a company, the leader at the top who sets the tone. The energy of the transiting planet is more like "your boss" at the company. You'll feel that "boss" energy and influence most, however the vibe of the higher level CEO or "planetary ruler" is always there.

And remember, while you likely relate most to your sun, moon, and rising signs—you'll see yourself in all of the signs as you look deeper into the intricacies of your birth chart and the current alignment of the cosmos.

It's also interesting to think of the zodiac signs as a progression as well as a cycle. Aries can represent the "youngest" of the signs, and Pisces can depict the oldest or wisest archetype.

01 ARIES

Aries is akin to the first day of spring. Aries' magic is starting new things fearlessly with a burst of energy. The shadow of Aries can be a lack of patience for finishing long-term projects and a bit of selfishness or unwillingness to listen to other people's experiences. Mars is a fitting planetary ruler for this sign, as it is all about taking action courageously. Since Aries starts off the spring, it is a cardinal sign. Astrologers categorize it as masculine and of the element of Fire. The sun is in Aries approximately March 21st - April 19th.

02 TAURUS

Taurus brings the energy down a notch, carefully considering which actions to take and moving slowly. The magic of Taurus is in grounding into the Earth, the pure power of existing just "to be." The shadow can come through in stubbornness or taking too little action, as well as a fixation on material things. Taurus's ruler is Venus, the planet of earthly pleasures. Taurus is a fixed sign (mid-season) and is feminine and of the Earth element. The sun is in Taurus from April 20th - May 20th.

03 GEMINI

Twinning! Gemini represents duality and the ability to be and understand "both sides" of the situation. Gemini's power is in communication and listening without judgment. The shadow of Gemini may manifest in inauthenticity or a tendency to be unfocused or flighty. Its planetary ruler is Mercury—the planet of the mind. Gemini is mutable as it falls at the end of the season. Astrologers classify it as masculine (although it represents duality), and it is of the Air element. The sun is in Gemini from May 21st - June 20th.

04 CANCER

Cancer's powers are in the comforts of home, routines, intuition, and the hidden realm of emotions. Therein lies the shadow, the tension between the strength of outer protection and the depths of inner sensitivity. Emotions can feel like "too much," however the shell can be overprotective, causing the crab to avoid vulnerability and hold themselves back. The moon rules Cancer. It is feminine, cardinal, and of the Water element. The sun is in Cancer from June 21st - July 22nd.

05 LEO

Rrawr!! Leo is all about creative expression of self. It is a reminder that even though you are a part of the larger universe, you are the star of your own show. Leo's magic is in shining light and creativity into the world. And remember, the brightest lights cast the strongest shadows. Leo energy can plummet into the abyss of moodiness and a disruptive dark-side when feeling unfulfilled or unloved. Leo is the sign of the sun, is fixed (center of the season), masculine, and of the Fire element. The sun is in Leo July 23rd - August 22nd.

06 VIRGO

If there is a sign that represents "dark academia," it is Virgo. Virgo is the perfectionist, the judge, the analyzer. Virgo works with mundane earthly matters, weaving the practical and mystical. Of course, the shadow of Virgo's perfectionism is... the perfectionism. Virgo is a cruel judge of their own inner light and can feel inadequate despite a high level of talent or education. The planet Mercury rules this sign, and it is feminine, mutable, and of the Earth element. The sun is in Virgo from August 23rd - September 22nd.

07 LIBRA

Represented by the scales of balance, Libra is the sign of harmony. While Gemini represents the duality of opposites, Libra is about balance and equilibrium. It is the sign of partnerships and social interactions. Under Libra's shadow, you may be too passive or too aggressive with others. Libra thrives in the middle, yet must remember to be decisive and bold enough to satisfy their own needs, too. Venus rules this sign and it is cardinal, masculine, and of the Air element. The sun is in Libra September 23rd - October 22nd.

08 SCORPIO

"I heard Scorpios are evil!" a small child said. No, my child. They're just... misunderstood. Scorpio represents the power of transformation through the dark of the unknown. It conveys pain, the sting of a barbed tail. Yet it also wields the energy to create change. Scorpio's wisdom lies in the capacity to channel power, magic, and psychic energy. Mars and Pluto (the planet of the underworld) rule Scorpio. It is feminine, fixed, and of the Water element. The sun is in Scorpio on October 23rd - November 21st.

09 SAGITTARIUS

Sagittarius's arrow represents focus, speed, and versatility. Jupiter gives it the powers of expansion, luck, and abundance. It doesn't matter where Sagittarius points their arrow, they will discover something valuable. The shadow comes out when they are too quick to shoot, becoming hotheaded, absentminded, or unreliable. Jupiter rules Sagittarius and it is masculine, mutable, and of the Fire element. The sun is in Sagittarius from November 22nd - December 21st.

10 CAPRICORN

Capricorn focuses on achieving dreams through a rock-solid structure and process. Capricorn's magic is the mastery of time, energy, and resources—reducing things to what's essential, then moving forward steadily to reach their goals. Capricorn's shadow lies in the tendency to act like a grumpy and skeptical goat, especially when faced with new ways of doing things. Saturn rules Capricorn and it is feminine, cardinal, and of the Earth. The sun is in Capricorn December 22nd - January 19th.

11 AQUARIUS

The only thing you can expect from Aquarius is the unexpected. Aquarius represents the outpouring of wisdom to change the world. Strategically detached from emotions, Aquarians may analyze feelings but tend to not take things personally. The eccentricity of Aquarius may cause detachment and the inability to let their ideas "flow." Saturn and Uranus (the planet of the unexpected) rule this sign, and it is masculine, fixed, and of the Air element. The sun is in Aquarius from January 20th - February 18th.

12 PISCES

The last sign in the cycle, Pisces represents maturity, enlightenment, and the harmony of our Earthly selves and the divine. Imagine Mister Rogers and the gentle ways he expresses deep topics and mysteries. The mastery of emotion and earthly presence is Pisces's gift. Contrarily, the shadow of Pisces is moody and mopey in a childlike way. Pisces may overindulge instead of dealing with their emotions in healthier ways. Neptune rules Pisces, and is feminine, mutable, and of the Water element. The sun is in Pisces February 19th - March 20th.

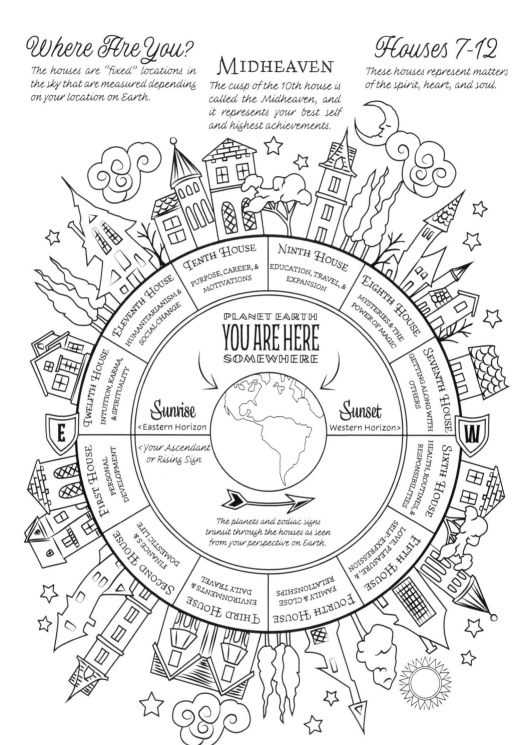

Where Are You?

The houses are "fixed" locations in the sky that are measured depending on your location on Earth.

MIDHEAVEN

The cusp of the 10th house is called the Midheaven, and it represents your best self and highest achievements.

Houses 7-12

These houses represent matters of the spirit, heart, and soul.

PLANET EARTH
YOU ARE HERE
SOMEWHERE

Sunrise
<Eastern Horizon
<Your Ascendant or Rising Sign

Sunset
Western Horizon>

The planets and zodiac signs transit through the houses as seen from your perspective on Earth.

TENTH HOUSE
PURPOSE, CAREER, & MOTIVATIONS

NINTH HOUSE
EDUCATION, TRAVEL, & EXPANSION

EIGHTH HOUSE
MYSTERIES & THE POWER OF MAGIC

ELEVENTH HOUSE
HUMANITARIANISM & SOCIAL CHANGE

SEVENTH HOUSE
GETTING ALONG WITH OTHERS

TWELFTH HOUSE
INTUITION, KARMA & SPIRITUALITY

SIXTH HOUSE
HEALTH, ROUTINES, & RESPONSIBILITIES

FIRST HOUSE
PERSONAL DEVELOPMENT

FIFTH HOUSE
LOVE, PLEASURE, & SELF-EXPRESSION

SECOND HOUSE
FINANCES & DOMESTIC LIFE

FOURTH HOUSE
FAMILY & CLOSE RELATIONSHIPS

THIRD HOUSE
ENVIRONMENTS & DAILY TRAVEL

Ascendant

Find the first house on the eastern horizon from where you are (or where you were). This is called the Ascendant or Rising Sign on your birth chart.

Houses 1-6

The first six houses represent "earthly" and mundane matters of life.

Descendant

The cusp of the 7th house on the western horizon is called the Descendant. It represents what you most admire in others.

THE 12 HOUSES

The houses show "where" planetary energies and zodiac traits are likely to emerge in daily life. Houses are where your motivations (planets) and personality (signs) interact with the world. Look at the houses in your birth chart and the positions of the cosmos today for practical advice on how to approach these areas of life.

While planets and signs are constantly in motion, houses don't move. However, we calculate the houses depending on *where you are on Earth*. Planets and signs move through the sky but are the same no matter where you are. Yet the houses depend on your location.

01 First House: You may have heard about your Ascendant or "Rising Sign." This refers to the first house—the zodiac sign on the eastern horizon at the time and place of your birth.

The first house relates to your personal development and innate personality. While your sun sign is about how YOU see yourself, the ascendant and first house is your persona or "mask"—how OTHERS see you. This house corresponds to Aries and Mars.

02 Second House: This house is the realm of self-esteem, security, and feelings of comfort and worth, as well as matters of domestic life, finances, and material possessions. The second house corresponds to Taurus and Venus.

03 Third House: The third house is about environments—your home, city, workplace, car, school, etc. It'll help you sense where you'll thrive or feel comfortable. It is also the house of daily transportation and short, practical trips. It corresponds to Gemini and Mercury.

04 Fourth House: Want to work on your family relationships, especially with your mother?! This house is about home life and relationships. Find clues about how and where you need to be vulnerable or put up boundaries (like the crab). It corresponds to Cancer and the moon.

05 Fifth House: This house is like a carnival that has all of your favorite things—crafts, hobbies, games, activities, and even love—whatever you like to do for pleasure. If you're bored, look here for clues about what you can do to ignite your inner fire and have some fun. It corresponds to Leo and the sun.

06 Sixth House: The house of practical magic, this one is all about healthy habits like diet, fitness, responsibilities, and daily routines. This house shows what will motivate you to do all the productive things you'll thank yourself for later. It corresponds to Virgo and Mercury.

07 Seventh House: This house is about collaborative partnerships, from roommates and coworkers to spouses and friends. Look here for clues on achieving harmony in working together and ways to get along. It corresponds to Libra and Venus.

08 Eighth House: Sex! Death! Inheritance! Witchcraft!!! All the juiciest stuff is here in the eighth house, the gateway to transformation. It's also the house of investigation and of delving deep into the mysteries of your subconscious, and corresponds to Scorpio, Mars, and Pluto.

09 Ninth House: This house is like a hall of higher learning. It encompasses long-distance travels and any type of worldly exploration that broadens the mind. The ninth house can point you in new, exciting directions. This house corresponds to Sagittarius and Jupiter.

10 Tenth House: The house of career aspirations will show what motivates you to achieve and how you can spend your time in alignment with what matters most to you. It also sheds light on how you relate to authority and corresponds to Capricorn and Saturn.

11 Eleventh House: This is the house of humanitarianism. It'll show how you and your network of friends and social ties can have a positive effect on culture and the world at large. It's about community, the flow of ideas, and how your perspectives and existence can change the world. It corresponds to Aquarius, Saturn, and Uranus.

12 Twelfth House: This house delves into the realm of mysteries, secrets, dreams, and the unknown. It holds potent clues to your shadow self and ways to step out of self-destructive patterns. We also know this house as the house of Karma or the house of God. It's a place of seclusion and can show you where to go deeper within. It corresponds to Pisces, Neptune, and Jupiter.

DRAW A CHART

At any point in time (like right now!) the planets, signs, and houses are all configured and aligned in a particular way. Astrologers call this "snapshot" of the stars a chart or radix.

Your "birth chart" is the snapshot of the stars on the day and time of your birth, but you could make an astrological chart of any time in the past, present, or future.

Calculating a chart from scratch is an involved mathematical process with more instructions than will fit in this book. But you can quickly pull your chart from a website. Astro-charts.com is a free chart-making resource, but there are many others, such as horoscopes.astro-seek.com, or treat yourself to a reading from a professional astrologer.

STEP 1: THE SIGNS IN THE HOUSES

To begin, note the numbered "pie slices" or houses on your chart and the ring on the outside. We draw the 1st house or Ascendant on the left, abbreviated with AC.

Write all twelve zodiac signs around the wheel counterclockwise, starting with the 1st house Ascendant and ending with the 12th house.

If your rising sign is Aquarius, the 11th sign of the zodiac, you'll write the word or symbol "Aquarius" in the 1st house Ascendant position. Then in the 2nd house, you'll write "Pisces," the 12th sign of the zodiac. In the 3rd house, Aries,

and so on until you've written out all twelve.

STEP 2: THE PLANETS

Once you've written all twelve signs in the houses—move on to the "planets" part of your birth chart, the second ring from the outside. You may not have planets in all of the houses, so some may be blank. Draw the symbol and/or name of each planet, noting the "degree" marks to pinpoint their locations.

STEP 3: THE ASPECTS

The aspects are the geometries and forces between the planets. Turn the page to read more about aspects, then come back and fill in at least the one or two major aspects you've researched in your own chart.

A NERDY NOTE ABOUT GENERATIONAL PLANETS: Outer planets with longer transits between signs will be the same for everyone born within several years of each other. Look to the house of these planets in your birth chart for more detail about your individual characteristics with these planets.

A NERDY NOTE ABOUT HOUSES: There are several ways to measure the houses. This book uses the "equal" house system because it's the most straightforward and "easy" to pick up. However, you may prefer and explore another house system.

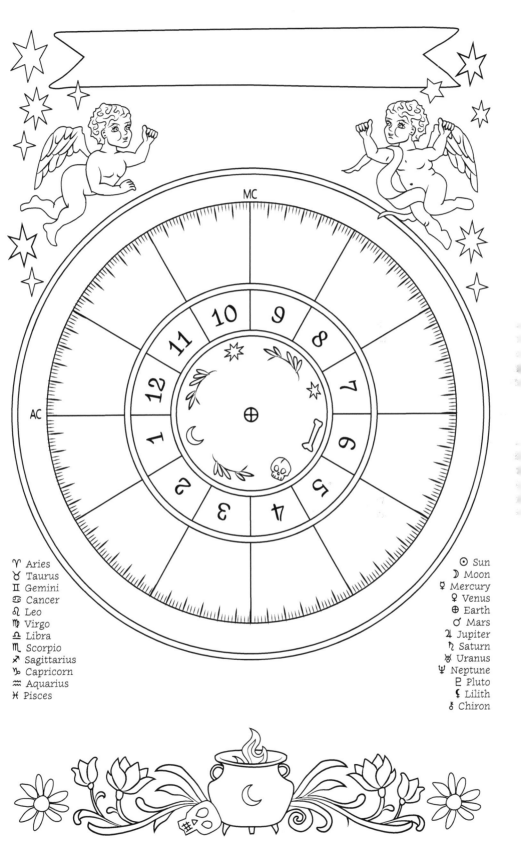

Aries ♈ Aries
♉ Taurus
♊ Gemini
♋ Cancer
♌ Leo
♍ Virgo
♎ Libra
♏ Scorpio
♐ Sagittarius
♑ Capricorn
♒ Aquarius
♓ Pisces

☉ Sun
☽ Moon
☿ Mercury
♀ Venus
⊕ Earth
♂ Mars
♃ Jupiter
♄ Saturn
♅ Uranus
♆ Neptune
♇ Pluto
⚸ Lilith
⚷ Chiron

SYNASTRY CHART

CHART 1 (OUTER RINGS)   CHART 2 (INNER RING)

ASPECTS BETWEEN THE CHARTS

< PLANETS FOR CHART 1 >

< PLANETS FOR CHART 2 >

AC

< ZODIAC SIGNS FOR CHART 1 STARTING WITH ASCENDANT (AC) 1ST HOUSE >

♈ Aries
♉ Taurus
♊ Gemini
♋ Cancer
♌ Leo
♍ Virgo
♎ Libra
♏ Scorpio
♐ Sagittarius
♑ Capricorn
♒ Aquarius
♓ Pisces

☉ Sun
☽ Moon
☿ Mercury
♀ Venus
♂ Mars
♃ Jupiter
♄ Saturn
♅ Uranus
♆ Neptune
♇ Pluto

PLANETARY ASPECTS

Aspects are the geometries and alignments that form between planets. These aspects intensify planetary energy, and the interactions that arise can be positive, negative, or neutral, depending on the alignment.

Check out the aspects (a series of lines and geometric shapes) in the center circle of your birth chart. How are the planets aligned with each other? Are they bunched up together? Are they balanced or opposite each other?

Think of the planets sort of like people. Jupiter is "expansive" and Saturn is "contractive," for example. They can either work together, maximizing their own strengths for the benefit of the whole, or there may be a tension of differences between the two opposites.

And just like working with people, you may not be able to change the planetary energy, but you can learn to work with it. If you know when planetary energies are intensified or butting heads, you can plan your own strategy to stay centered and in your power.

CONJUNCTION ♂

When planets are together or in conjunction within a few degrees of each other, their energies are intensified.

SEXTILE ✳

A sextile or 60° angle between planets brings about a lovely exchange of harmony and flowing energy.

OPPOSITION ☍

An opposition or 180° angle between planets can cause tension, or it can create a harmonious polarity or duality.

SQUARE ☐

A square or 90° angle between planets causes tension which can typically be resolved with a little compromise.

TRINE △

A trine or 120° angle is the aspect of luck and fortuitous energies. The gate is open and magic is flowing your way.

SYNASTRY

Astrologers use synastry to compare two charts—overlaying them to see what patterns and energies arise. Typically, "synastry" refers to romantic pairings, but you could use your birth chart and today's date to see the energies between yourself and the current planetary alignments. Or you could compare your birth chart and the birth chart of a friend or lover, or to any day and time in the past or future.

You can compare charts to get clarity on how celestial energies affected you when you had significant events in your past. Or you can use this method to plan for "big" days ahead.

Make a synastry chart on the left between yourself and another person or time. Use a synastry chart generator like astro-charts.com or horoscopes.astro-seek.com, then copy it over and see what you can uncover within the planetary aspects. This is an "advanced" topic, so if it's confusing, not to worry! Take your time and use tools, books, and astrologers to help you out as needed.

THE MOON IN THE ZODIAC

The moon influences the unconscious and emotional energies on Earth, so everyone—no matter their personal moon sign—feels the influence of the moon's shenanigans. You'll often hear the moon sign called out (full moon in Scorpio!) and the moon's transits are noted on the weekly calendars pages that follow. Use this page as a handy reference sheet to feel out the intricacies of the moon as it transits and cycles through the zodiac signs.

Our moon travels through the zodiac in 28 days and switches signs every two or three days.

ARIES ♈ A desire to start fresh. Energy for starting short-term projects. Not the best time for long-term planning.

TAURUS ♉ The sign of the home, comfort, decor, and finances. An optimal moon sign for starting long-term projects.

GEMINI ♊ A time for thinking, learning, reading, pursuing curiosities and interests, doing mental activities, and talking to fascinating people.

CANCER ♋ An auspicious time to be at home, reflect, and get in touch with your feelings. A time to focus on family and love.

LEO ♌ The sign of the self and creativity. A magical time to get in touch with your own intuition and listen for what your heart truly desires.

VIRGO ♍ Organization, efficient habits, and health. The best time to start a routine or positive habit, organize, get on a schedule, or tidy things up.

LIBRA ♎ The sign of diplomacy, balance, and visual appeal. A good time to work on relationships, find balance, and socialize.

SCORPIO ♏ A good time to "find" motivation, harness your own power, take control, and rid yourself of things that no longer serve you.

SAGITTARIUS ♐ The sign of truth and visions. This is an auspicious time to make long-term plans, think big, use your imagination, and visualize a positive future.

CAPRICORN ♑ A time to focus on career, business, structure, careful use of resources, and practical achievement.

AQUARIUS ♒ The sign of esoterica, freethinking, and personal freedom. A good time to expand your mind to find new, unexpected ideas and solutions.

PISCES ♓ The sign of dreaming, psychic awareness, and intuition. An auspicious time for divination, reflection, mystical pursuits, and retreating into nature or water.

VOID-OF-COURSE MOON

There are void-of-course spots in between the moon signs. In these transitional phases, when the moon is void of course, there is a period of low energy where you may feel drained and exhausted or have trouble making decisions. Stores and businesses are "unusually" quiet, and people experience difficulty working together. It's also best not to start new projects or meet new people during the moon's void-of-course.

Often, you don't notice any difference because the void of course can be short—just a couple of minutes. But sometimes these periods can be hours or days, and that's when the shift in energy is quite noticeable! Being aware of these spots will help you use this energy to your advantage.

To see where these void spots are on the weekly calendar pages, look for the black triangles: ▶ These black triangles mark the start of the moon void-of-course cycle. The void ends when the moon enters the next sign.

PLANETARY RETROGRADES

Retrogrades happen when the planets appear to be moving backwards in our sky. When this occurs, planetary energy may have the opposite effect as "normal," causing confusion, a sudden change of perspective, or a need to "re-look," "re-bel," or "re-treat" in their area of planetary influence. These occurrences are marked on the calendar pages, as it can be helpful to be aware of their possible effects.

MERCURY: Mercury rules communication, so you may experience problems with technology, messages, or conversations. When Mercury is retrograde, back up, double-check, and be extra careful with what you say and hear. Prepare to be confused.

VENUS: Venus rules love and beauty. Be cautious about romantic relationships, exes, and changes in your physical appearance during Venus retrograde. Don't make a drastic change in your hair or sudden decisions with love.

MARS: Mars rules power and success. Don't start something big and new when Mars is retrograde. Make sure to think through career or business decisions. You may feel particularly slow or unenergized.

JUPITER: Jupiter rules travel, expansion, higher education, and finance. During Jupiter retrograde you may have issues with transportation or trouble making progress or "growing" your career and finances. It's a good time to slow down, make sure not to overspend, and to take time to learn, study, and experiment.

SATURN: Saturn rules responsibility, structure, and discipline, and is often an illuminator of limitations. When Saturn goes retrograde, it gives you an opportunity to move past failure and see beyond boundaries and comfort zones.

NEPTUNE: Neptune rules illusion, dreams, spirituality, and fantasy. As these influences disappear during a retrograde, you may feel the stark reality of things you normally do not see. Use this time to re-look at the truth versus what you've been telling yourself and find clues on how to bring dreams to reality.

URANUS: Uranus rules the unexpected, things involving change, liberation, and innovation. Uranus retrograde can push you to big realizations, where you can see past your limitations and fears. This retrograde can show you where you need to make changes.

PLUTO: Pluto rules the shadow and the underworld. During a Pluto retrograde, look at your shadow self and your needs for recognition, authority, and power. It's a good time to discover your shadow and find ways to work through the darkness.

PLANETARY RETROGRADES (℞) IN 2022:

Uranus ℞ begins August 19, 2021 and ends January 18, 2022.
Venus ℞ begins December 19, 2021 and ends January 29th, 2022.
Mercury ℞ begins January 14, 2022 and ends February 3, 2022.
Pluto ℞ begins April 29, 2022 and ends October 8, 2022.
Mercury ℞ begins May 10, 2022 and ends June 3, 2022.
Saturn ℞ begins June 4, 2022 and ends October 23, 2022.

Neptune ℞ begins June 28, 2022 and ends December 3, 2022.
Jupiter ℞ begins July 28, 2022 and ends November 23, 2022.
Uranus ℞ begins August 24, 2022 and ends January 22, 2023.
Mercury ℞ begins September 9, 2022 and ends October 2, 2022.
Mars ℞ begins October 30, 2022 and ends January 12, 2023.
Mercury ℞ begins December 29, 2022 and ends January 18, 2023.

ECLIPSES

Eclipses happen when the sun or moon appears "blacked out" by a celestial shadow.

Eclipses always come in pairs and opposite signs. A lunar eclipse in Taurus will follow a solar eclipse in Scorpio, for example.

A total lunar eclipse always coincides with a full moon and typically marks an energetic ending or culmination point. A total solar eclipse always coincides with the new moon and signifies a shift towards new beginnings.

If an eclipse's sign coincides with your own moon, rising, or sun sign—get ready for exciting events and turning points in your life.

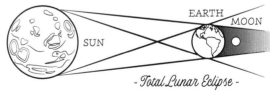

- Total Lunar Eclipse -

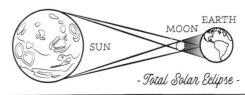

- Total Solar Eclipse -

ECLIPSES IN 2022:
Partial Solar Eclipse ♉ April 30
Total Lunar Eclipse ♏ May 16

Partial Solar Eclipse ♏ October 25
Total Lunar Eclipse ♉ November 8

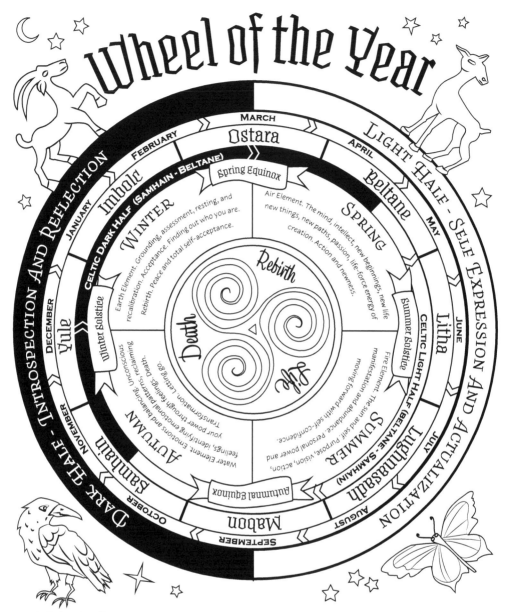

WORKING WITH THE CYCLES OF THE EARTH AND MOON

Astrology looks at what's happening outside of our planet, but the seasons or the "Wheel of the Year" relate to the cycles, tilt, and planetary motion right here on Earth.

Ancient Celts celebrated these seasonal shifts and used them for magic and ritual, as noted on the chart above and the spells within.

The phase of the moon is another intricacy of energetic life on Earth. The moon is our closest celestial neighbor and is a "tidally locked" satellite that orbits around us.

The moon's reflected sunlight and energetic subtleties can help you ebb and flow with your own magical cycles and powers.

A Note About the Cross Quarter Dates: The dates for the two solstices and two equinoxes each year—Ostara, Litha, Mabon, and Yule—are calculated astronomically, from the position of the Earth to the sun. The "cross quarter" festivals, which are the points between —Imbolc, Beltane, Lughnasadh, and Samhain—are often celebrated on "fixed" dates instead of the actual midpoints. And so, this book lists both the "Fixed Festival Dates" where it's more common to celebrate, and the "Astronomical Dates". Choose either date or any time in between for your own festivities or ritual. 'Tis the season for magic.

Moon Phases

New Moon
SET NEW INTENTIONS
Start New Projects
Renew & Regenerate

Crescent
BEGINNINGS
Creativity & Exploration
Transformation

1st Quarter
TAKING ACTION
Increasing Energy
Drawing Things In

Gibbous
DEVELOPMENT
Positive Affirmations
Moving Forward

Full Moon
CULMINATION
Release the Past
Complete & Fulfill

Disseminating
GRATITUDE & THANKS
Clarity of Purpose
New Knowledge

Last Quarter
BANISHING
Letting Things Go
Stopping Bad Habits

Balsamic
REFLECTION
What've You Learned?
Looking Inward

Dark Moon
REST
Solitude & Meditation
Shadow Work

NEW MOON
WAXING
FULL MOON
WANING

YOUR COSMIC YEAR

So are you ready to align with the cosmos and be the best witch you can be? Yes? Good call.

Here is a cosmic worksheet to help you get started. Use a "Transit Chart" calculator from a site like horoscopes.astro-seek.com to fill in the information below. And of course, this is the "coloring book" version of astrology—there is so much more to know about how the planets interact with your chart. Seek out information on your own or hire an astrologer to learn more.

TRANSITS OF THE OUTER PLANETS IN 2022:

These planets make big, slow transits and represent major phases and chapters of your life. When do these planets "return" to their positions on your birth chart? And where do the transits in 2022 appear in relation to your chart?

Your Next Mars Return (2 years) _____
Your Next Jupiter Return (12 years) _____
Your Next Saturn Return (29 years) _____
Your Next Uranus Return (84 years) _____

TRANSIT DATE & SIGN: *HOUSE & SIGN IN YOUR CHART:*

Jupiter enters Aries May 11, 2022: _____

Saturn is in Aquarius until 2023: _____

Pluto is in Capricorn until 2023: _____

Neptune is in Pisces until 2025: _____

Uranus is in Taurus until 2025: _____

ASPECTS OF THE OUTER & INNER PLANETS:

Are the transiting outer planets coming into notable aspects with the inner planets in your birth chart?

	SUN	MOON	MERCURY	VENUS	MARS	OUTER PLANETS
Tr. Jupiter						
Tr. Saturn						
Tr. Uranus						
Tr. Neptune						
Tr. Pluto						

ASTROLOGY BY MONTH

For each month, review your yearly outlook and the following cosmic tidbits.

Use a "Transit Chart" calculator from a site like horoscopes.astro-seek.com.

THE MOON: Evaluate the energy of the new and full moons for the month, and get your bearings on how these moons coordinate with the things you want to do.

● *What house and sign does the new moon fall in your birth chart? What do you want to grow?*

● *What house and sign does the full moon fall in your birth chart? What do you want to release or empower?*

THE SUN: Note the sun sign change for the month, and what house and sign the sun transits through in your chart. *What kind of seasonal energy are you feeling?*

THE INNER PLANETS: Notice the sign changes in Mercury, Venus, and Mars. These inner planets change signs every month or two.

Mercury will give you clues to the flow of energy and to your mental outlook. Venus will give you hints to what you'll need and desire. And Mars will offer insight into your drive and capacity for action.

● *Note if sign changes are happening for Mercury, Venus, and Mars, and which house and sign they fall in your birth chart.*

AND MORE: Look ahead to see if any eclipses, retrogrades, or sabbat celebrations are coming up, and how these might relate to your current goals or intentions.

How can you use these cosmic energies to your advantage and work in harmony with them?

ASTROLOGY BY DAY

It's nice to stay connected! Look up and find the moon and sun in the sky every day if you can.

1. MOON SIGN: Note the moon sign or moon void-of-course each day.

2. MOON PHASE: Note the phase of the moon. Is it waxing, waning, full, or new? How do you feel as the moon cycles from new to full and back?

3. ASPECTS TO THE MOON: If you want to go further, research what aspects the moon currently has to the other transiting planets.

4. LUNAR OR SOLAR POWERED? How do you relate to the rise and set of the sun and moon?

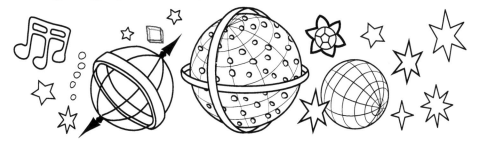

Spellcasting Basics

There are opening and closing steps that are basic accompaniments to spells in this book. These steps are optional but advisable: at least know "why" many witches perform these processes and try them out for yourself.

And keep in mind, this is a super basic "coloring book" guide to the spellcasting process. There are books and online sources that go much further in-depth.

THE SECRET OF SPELLS

The secret to powerful spells is in you. Your feeling and vibration in alignment with your true source of self—or a higher power—is what makes spells work.

The secret isn't in having the right ingredients and doing all the steps in a particular order. It's in your ability to focus your intent and use your feelings, mind, and soul to call in what you want—to harness the energy of yourself in harmony with the Earth, stars, moon, planets, or whatever other spiritual forces you call upon.

BREAK THE RULES

The first rule is to throw out any of the rules that don't work for you. Do things that feel right, significant, and meaningful. Adapt spells from different practices, books, and teachers. The only way to know what works is to follow your curiosity and try things out.

USING TOOLS

Your feelings and vibration are what make the magic, not the tools, exact words, or sequences. You can cast amazing spells for free with no tools at all, and you can cast an elaborate spell that yields no results.

That said, tools like herbs, oils, crystals, and cauldrons can be powerful and fun to use in your spells. Just don't feel pressured or discouraged if you don't have much to start. Keep your magic straightforward and powerful. The right tools and ingredients will come.

"AS ABOVE, SO BELOW"

Tools, ingredients, and symbols are based on the magical theory of sympathetic magic and correspondence. You might hear the phrase, "As Above, So Below," which means the spiritual qualities of objects are passed down to earth. It's "sympathetic magic," or "this equals that," like how a figure of a lion represents that power but is not an actual lion.

Start by following lists, charts, and spells to get a feel for what others use and then begin to discover your own meaningful symbolism and correspondences.

PERMISSION

Spellbooks are like guidelines. They should be modified, simplified, or embellished to your liking. And don't degrade your magic by calling it "lazy." Keeping your witchcraft simple is okay. Go ahead, you have permission.

Also, it's not a competition to see who can use the most esoteric stuff in their spell. Hooray! It's about finding your personal power and style.

SPELLCASTING OUTLINE:

1. Plan and prepare.
2. Cast a circle.
3. Ground and center.
4. Invoke a deity or connection to self.
5. Raise energy.
6. Do your spellcraft (like the spells in this book).
7. Ground and center again.
8. Close your circle.
9. Clean up.
10. Act in accord (and be patient!).

1. PLAN AND PREPARE: If you're doing a written spell, read it several times to get familiar with it. Decide if there's anything you'll substitute or change. If you're writing your own spell, enjoy the process and mystery of seeing the messages and theme come together.

Gather all of the items you'll be using (if any) and plan out space and time where you'll do the spell. Spells can be impromptu, so preparations can be quick and casual if you like.

2. CAST A CIRCLE AND CALL THE QUARTERS: A magic circle is a container to collect the energy of your spell. Circles are also protective, as they form a ring or "barrier" around you. Circles can elevate your space to a higher vibration and clear out unwanted energy before you begin. Calling the Quarters is done to get the universal energy of the elements flowing. Incense is typically burned at the same time to purify the air and energy. If you

can't burn things, that's ok. If you've never cast a circle, try it. It's a mystical experience like no other. Once you have a few candles lit and start to walk around it, magic does happen!

HOW TO CAST A CIRCLE: This is a basic, bare-bones way to cast a circle. It's often much more elaborate, and this explanation barely does it justice, so read up to find out more. And note that while some cast the circle first and then call the Quarters, some do it the other way around.

1. Hold out your hand, wand, or crystal, and imagine a white light and a sphere of pure energy surrounding your space, as you circle around clockwise three times. Your circle can be large or it can be tiny, just space for you and your materials.

2. Call the Four Quarters or Five Points of the Pentagram, depending on your preferences. The Quarters (also known as the Elements!) are Earth (North), Air (East), Fire (South), and Water (West). Many use the Pentagram and also call the 5th Element, Spirit or Self.

Face in each direction and say a few words to welcome the element. For example, "To the North, I call upon your power of grounding and strength. To the East, I call upon the source of knowledge. To the South, I call upon your passion and burning desire to take action. To the West, I call upon the intuition of emotion. To the Spirit and Source of Self, I call upon your guidance and light."

3. GROUND AND CENTER: Grounding and centering prepare you to use the energy from the Earth, elements, and universe. Most witches agree that if you skip these steps, you'll be drawing off of your own energy, which can be exhausting and ineffective. It's wise to ground and center both before and after a spell. It's like the difference between being "plugged into" the magical energy of the Earth and universe versus "draining your batteries."

HOW TO GROUND AND CENTER:

To ground, imagine the energy coming up from the core of the Earth and into your feet, as you breathe deeply. You can visualize deep roots from your feet all the way into the center of the Earth, with these roots drawing the Earth's energy in and out of you. The point is to allow these great channels of energy to flow through you and into your spell. You can also imagine any of your negative energy, thoughts, or stress leaving.

To center, once you've got a good flow of energy from the ground, imagine the energy shining through and out the top of your head as a pure form of your highest creative self and then back in as the light of guidance. Suspend yourself here between the Earth and the sky, supported with the energy flowing freely through you, upheld, balanced, cleansed, and "in flow" with the energy of the universe. This process takes just a couple of minutes.

4. INVOKE A DEITY OR CREATIVE SOURCE: If you'd like to invoke a deity or your highest self to help raise energy and your vibration, call upon them. Invoking deities is way deeper than this book, so research it more if it calls to you!

5. RAISE ENERGY: The point of raising energy is to channel the universal (magical!) forces you tapped into through the previous steps to use in your spell. And raising energy is fun. You can sing, dance, chant, meditate, or do breath work. You want to do something that feels natural, so you can really get into it, lose yourself, and raise your state of consciousness.

A good way to start is to chant "Ong," allowing the roof of your mouth to vibrate ever so slightly. This vibration changes up the energy in your mind, body, and breath and is a simple yet powerful technique.

Another tip is to raise energy to the point of the "peak" where you feel it at its highest. Don't go too far where you start to tucker out or lose enthusiasm!

6. DO YOUR SPELL: Your spell can be as simple as saying an intention and focusing on achieving the outcome of what you want, or it can be more elaborate. Whichever way you prefer, do what feels right to you.

TIPS ON VISUALIZATION AND INTENTION:

Most spellwork involves a bit of imagination and intention, and here are some subtleties you can explore.

The Power of You The most important tool in magic is you. You've got it—both power right now and vast untapped power that you can explore. To cast a successful spell, you've got to focus your mind and genuinely feel the emotions and feelings of the things you want to manifest.

If you haven't started meditating in some form yet, start now! It's not too late, and it's easier than you think.

Visualize the Outcome

Visualization doesn't have to be visual. In fact, *feeling* the outcome of what you want may be more effective than seeing it (try both). And try to feel or see the *completion* of your desire without worrying about the process or *how* you'll get there.

If you don't know how you're going to achieve your goal (yet!) it can feel overwhelming when you try to visualize how you're going to pull it off. Instead, feel the sense of calm, completion, and control that you'll feel *after* you achieve it.

Phrase it Positively

Another tip is to phrase your intentions and desires positively. You're putting energy into this, so make sure the intention is going to be good for you. Instead of saying what you don't want, "to get out of my bad job that I hate," phrase it positively, "I want to do something that's fulfilling with my career."

Then you'll be able to feel good about it as you visualize and cast your spell.

7. GROUND AND CENTER AGAIN

After your spell, it's important to ground out any excess energy. Do this again by visualizing energy flowing through you and out. You can also imagine any "extra" energy you have petering out as you release it back into the Earth.

8. CLOSE YOUR CIRCLE

If you called the Quarters or a deity, let them know the spell has ended by calling them out again, with thanks if desired.

Close your circle the opposite of how you opened it, circling around three times or more counterclockwise. Then say, "This circle is closed," or do a closing chant or song to finish your spell.

9. CLEAN UP

Don't be messy with your magic! Put away all of your spell items.

10. ACT IN ACCORD: Once you have cast your spell, you've got to take action. You can cast a spell to become a marine biologist, but if you don't study for it, it's never going to happen. So take action towards what you want to open the possibility for it to come.

Look for signs, intuition, and coincidences that point you in the direction of your desires. If you get inspired after a spell, take action! Don't be surprised if you ask for money and then come up with a new idea to make money. Follow those clues, especially if they feel exciting and good.

If your spell comes true, discard and "release" any charm bag, poppet, or item you used to hold and amplify energy. Also, give thanks (if that's in your practice) or repay the universe in some way, doing something kind or of service that you feel is a solid trade for what you received from your spell.

WHAT IF YOUR SPELL DOESN'T WORK?

It's true that not all spells will work! But sometimes the results just take longer than you'd like, so be patient.

If your spell doesn't work, you can use divination or meditation to do some digging into reasons why.

The good news is your own magic, power, frequency, and intention is still on your side. You can try again and add more energy in the direction of your desired outcome by casting another spell.

Give it some deep thought. What else is at play? Did you really take inspired action? Are you totally honest with yourself about what you want? Are there any thoughts or feelings about your spell that feel "off"? Are you grateful for what you already have? Can you "give back" or reciprocate with service or energy?

FOR MORE TIPS AND INSPIRATION:

Seek out websites, books, podcasts, and videos on spirituality. Follow your intuition and curiosity to deepen your practice and find your own style. And check out other books in the *Coloring Book of Shadows* series, like the *Book of Spells* and *Witch Life*.

"Ⴧhe Zodiacal Laws of Ⴧhis Solar System"

An interpretation of Gibbs Mason's illustration in *She: The Woman-Man*, 1935, Aleta B. Baker

1ST HALF 2022

January

S	M	T	W	Th	F	Sa
						1
●	3	4	5	6	7	8
◑	10	11	12	13	14	15
16	○	18	19	20	21	22
23	24	◐	26	27	28	29
30	31					

February

S	M	T	W	Th	F	Sa
	●	2	3	4	5	
6	7	◑	9	10	11	12
13	14	15	○	17	18	19
20	21	22	◐	24	25	26
27	28					

March

S	M	T	W	Th	F	Sa
		1	●	3	4	5
6	7	8	9	◑	11	12
13	14	15	16	17	○	19
20	21	22	23	24	◐	26
27	28	29	30	31		

April

S	M	T	W	Th	F	Sa
					●	2
3	4	5	6	7	8	◑
10	11	12	13	14	15	○
17	18	19	20	21	22	◐
24	25	26	27	28	29	●

May

S	M	T	W	Th	F	Sa
1	2	3	4	5	6	7
◑	9	10	11	12	13	14
15	○	17	18	19	20	21
◐	23	24	25	26	27	28
29	●	31				

June

S	M	T	W	Th	F	Sa
			1	2	3	4
5	6	◑	8	9	10	11
12	13	○	15	16	17	18
19	◐	21	22	23	24	25
26	27	●	29	30		

2ND HALF 2022

July

S	M	T	W	Th	F	Sa
					1	2
3	4	5	◑	7	8	9
10	11	12	○	14	15	16
17	18	19	◐	21	22	23
24	25	26	27	●	29	30
31						

August

S	M	T	W	Th	F	Sa
	1	2	3	4	◐	6
7	8	9	10	○	12	13
14	15	16	17	18	◐	20
21	22	23	24	25	26	●
28	29	30	31			

September

S	M	T	W	Th	F	Sa
				1	2	◑
4	5	6	7	8	9	○
11	12	13	14	15	16	◐
18	19	20	21	22	23	24
●	26	27	28	29	30	

October

S	M	T	W	Th	F	Sa
						1
◑	3	4	5	6	7	8
○	10	11	12	13	14	15
16	◐	18	19	20	21	22
23	24	●	26	27	28	29
30	31					

November

S	M	T	W	Th	F	Sa
		◑	2	3	4	5
6	7	○	9	10	11	12
13	14	15	◐	17	18	19
20	21	22	●	24	25	26
27	28	29	◐			

December

S	M	T	W	Th	F	Sa
				1	2	3
4	5	6	○	8	9	10
11	12	13	14	15	◑	17
18	19	20	21	22	●	24
25	26	27	28	◑	30	31

INTUITION | REFLECTION | INTENTIONS | IMPORTANT THINGS | GOALS

Capricorn's Bag of Tricks

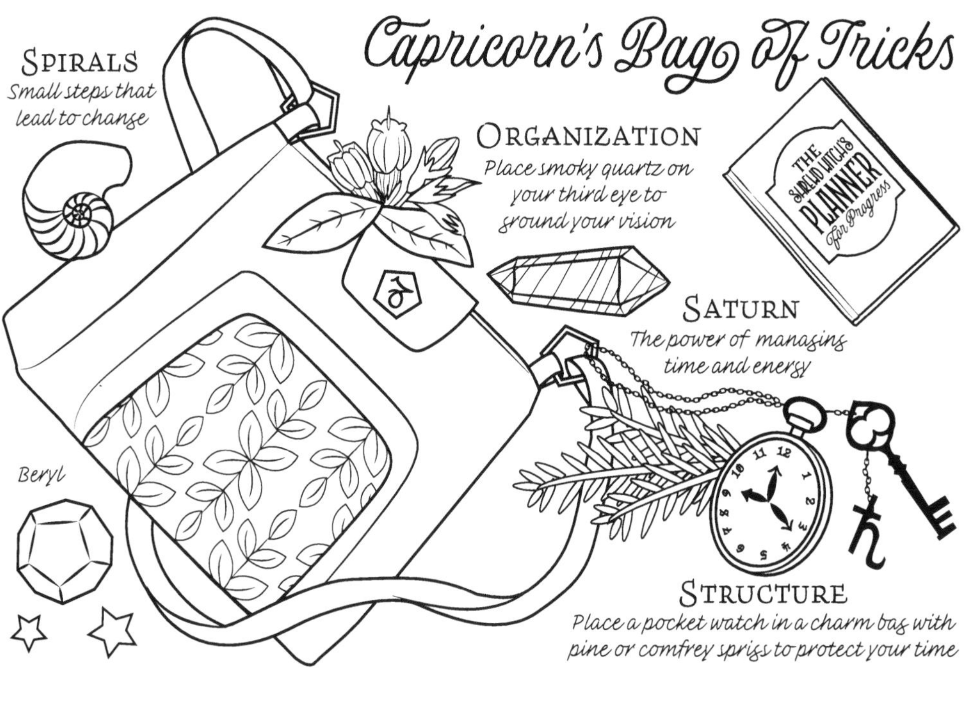

SPIRALS
Small steps that lead to change
ORGANIZATION
Place smoky quartz on your third eye to ground your vision
THE SHREWD WITCH'S PLANNER For Progress
SATURN
The power of managing time and energy
Beryl
STRUCTURE
Place a pocket watch in a charm bag with pine or comfrey sprigs to protect your time

Saturn - Cardinal - Earth - "I Utilize"

Hemlock
Focused Power

Belladonna
Banishing

CAPRICORN

THE MAGIC OF STABILITY & FOCUS

NEW & WAXING MOON: Choose a goal to focus on and begin taking steps towards it
FULL MOON: Channel your confidence and belief in yourself, then plan for your success
WANING & DARK MOON: Decide what's most important to achieve and let go of the rest

Pansies are pensive, yet down-to-earth. Place dried pansies on your altar or between the pages of your planner.

JANUARY

SACRED FOCUS
AN ALTAR TO STAND FIRMLY ON YOUR PATH

NOTE: If you do this spell outside of your home or garden, make sure to "leave no trace" and put the rocks back exactly where you found them. Never disturb ancient rock formations or Cairns.

There is power in structure, and Capricorn's magic is found there—reducing things to what's essential, then moving forward steadily.

One of the big "secrets" to the magic of time is that you create more time by doing less. Your focus is sacred and powerful.

ABOUT THE SPELL: Many ancient cultures stacked rocks for practical and spiritual purposes. The Celts created rock formations called Cairns as monuments to lives lost, dedications to causes, altars for prayers, and as essential trail markers.

In this spell, you'll build a stack of items on your altar to gain a steady foothold on your path.

PREPARE: Pick three to six big things that you want to focus on. Contract your list. Less is more—like a Capricorn. Examples: Health. Magic. Family. Money. Creativity. Find the least amount of things that are most important to you.

Gather items to stack that represent your areas of focus—use rocks, sea glass, books, teacups—whatever is meaningful (and stackable) for you.

CAST THE SPELL: Decide which is the base rock. What will topple the whole pile if it isn't steady? Place that rock at the center. Then stack the rest of your items, dedicating yourself to narrow your vision and focus as you go.

As your year passes, use this stack to pull your focus back on track. Meditate with the individual items for guidance, or switch out and re-stack them if you need to make a shift.

JANUARY 2022

	SUNDAY	MONDAY	TUESDAY
	26 Last Quarter ◑	27	28
	2 New Moon ● ♑	3	4
	9 First Quarter ◐	10	11
	16	17 Full Moon ○ ♋	Uranus Retrograde Ends 18
	23	24	25 Last Quarter ◑
	30	31	★ Imbolc (Fixed Date) 1 New Moon ● ♒

Wednesday	Thursday	Friday	Saturday
29	30	31	1
5	6	7	8
12	13	Mercury Retrograde Begins (ends Feb. 3rd) 14	15
☉ Sun in Aquarius ≈ 19	20	21	22
26	27	28	Venus Retrograde Ends 29
2	Mercury Retrograde Ends ★ Imbolc 3:37 PM EST 3	4	5

JANUARY 2022

MONDAY, DECEMBER 27, 2021

TUESDAY, DECEMBER 28, 2021
▸ Moon void-of-course begins 4:11 PM EST
Moon enters Scorpio ♏ 4:16 PM EST

WEDNESDAY, DECEMBER 29, 2021

THURSDAY, DECEMBER 30, 2021
▸ Moon void-of-course begins 12:10 PM EST
Moon enters Sagittarius ♐ 6:08 PM EST

FRIDAY, DECEMBER 31, 2021

SATURDAY, JANUARY 1
▸ Moon void-of-course begins 3:16 AM EST
Moon enters Capricorn ♑ 6:02 PM EST

SUNDAY, JANUARY 2
New Moon ● in Capricorn ♑ 1:33 PM EST

- Garnet -
Taking the time to
know yourself

- Poplar -
Trusting Yourself to Fly

- Lead -
The power
to transform

Capricorn & Saturn
FOCUSING YOUR VISION

JANUARY 2022

MONDAY, JANUARY 3
▸ Moon void-of-course begins 11:20 AM EST
Moon enters Aquarius ≈ 5:44 PM EST

TUESDAY, JANUARY 4
▸ Moon void-of-course begins 7:45 PM EST

WEDNESDAY, JANUARY 5
Moon enters Pisces ♓ 7:17 PM EST

THURSDAY, JANUARY 6

FRIDAY, JANUARY 7
▸ Moon void-of-course begins 5:23 PM EST

SATURDAY, JANUARY 8
Moon enters Aries ♈ 12:26 AM EST

SUNDAY, JANUARY 9
First Quarter ◑ 1:11 PM

TURQUOISE
How can I dissolve patterns of self-sabotage?

AMETHYST
Where can I benefit from moderation?

QUARTZ
How can I focus to make my life easier?

Gaze at Saturn through leaded glass

JANUARY 2022

MONDAY, JANUARY 10
► Moon void-of-course begins 2:23 AM EST
Moon enters Taurus ♉ 9:47 AM EST

TUESDAY, JANUARY 11

WEDNESDAY, JANUARY 12
► Moon void-of-course begins 2:39 PM EST
Moon enters Gemini ♊ 10:08 PM EST

THURSDAY, JANUARY 13

FRIDAY, JANUARY 14
► Moon void-of-course begins 9:22 PM EST
☿℞ Mercury Retrograde 6:41 AM EST - Feb. 3rd

SATURDAY, JANUARY 15
Moon enters Cancer ♋ 11:11 AM EST

SUNDAY, JANUARY 16

EARTH
THE ELEMENT OF BELONGING

JANUARY 2022

MONDAY, JANUARY 17
► Moon void-of-course begins 6:48 PM EST
Full Moon ○ in Cancer ♋ 6:48 PM EST
Moon enters Leo ♌ 11:02 PM EST

TUESDAY, JANUARY 18
♅℞ Uranus Retrograde ends 10:26 AM EST

WEDNESDAY, JANUARY 19
☉ Sun enters Aquarius ♒ 9:38 PM EST

THURSDAY, JANUARY 20
► Moon void-of-course begins 3:15 AM EST
Moon enters Virgo ♍ 9:02 AM EST

FRIDAY, JANUARY 21

SATURDAY, JANUARY 22
► Moon void-of-course begins 2:46 PM EST
Moon enters Libra ♎ 5:02 PM EST

SUNDAY, JANUARY 23

EARTH WITCHERY

- Work with plants, animals, or crystals and spend time in nature.
- Sprinkle salt or place selenite at the four corners of your home or altar.
- Meditate facing north, imagining roots growing from you into the ground.
- Work with a mantra like, "I know and trust myself."
- Burn an earthy incense like patchouli, cypress, or vetivert.

JANUARY 2022

MONDAY, JANUARY 24
▸ Moon void-of-course begins 5:10 PM EST
Moon enters Scorpio ♏ 10:57 PM EST

TUESDAY, JANUARY 25
Last Quarter ◑ 8:41 AM EST

WEDNESDAY, JANUARY 26

THURSDAY, JANUARY 27
▸ Moon void-of-course begins 12:28 AM EST
Moon enters Sagittarius ♐ 2:34 AM EST

FRIDAY, JANUARY 28
▸ Moon void-of-course begins 2:00 PM EST

SATURDAY, JANUARY 29
♀℞ Venus Retrograde ends 3:46 AM EST
Moon enters Capricorn ♑ 4:09 AM EST

SUNDAY, JANUARY 30
▸ Moon void-of-course begins 11:44 PM EST

- Earthen Vessels -
Transmutation of the Elements

JANUARY/FEBRUARY 2022

MONDAY, JANUARY 31
Moon enters Aquarius ≈ 4:44 AM EST

TUESDAY, FEBRUARY 1
★ Imbolc (Fixed Festival Date)
New Moon ● in Aquarius ≈ 12:46 AM EST
▶ Moon void-of-course begins 6:01 AM EST

WEDNESDAY, FEBRUARY 2
Moon enters Pisces ♓ 5:59 AM EST

THURSDAY, FEBRUARY 3
★ Imbolc (Astronomical Date) 3:37 PM EST
☿℞ Mercury Retrograde ends 11:13 PM EST

FRIDAY, FEBRUARY 4
▶ Moon void-of-course begins 4:41 AM EST
Moon enters Aries ♈ 9:56 AM EST

SATURDAY, FEBRUARY 5

SUNDAY, FEBRUARY 6
▶ Moon void-of-course begins 12:21 PM EST
Moon enters Taurus ♉ 5:53 PM EST

Give offerings of herbs, corn,
or natural materials for
weaving and craftings

GRANDMOTHER SPIDER
NATIVE AMERICAN GODDESS OF EARTH & CREATION

Aquarius's Bag of Tricks

HUMANITARIAN
*Make waves and lead change
to help humanity evolve*

URANUS
*Think of a radical
change that you wish
to make*

UNIQUE
*Tend to an orchid
to enhance your
unique magic*

CONSCIOUS
*Carry rainbow fluorite to enhance
your link to universal consciousness*

OPTIMISTIC
*Drink cherry blossom tea
to renew your faith in humanity*

Uranus - Fixed - Air - "I Change"

AQUARIUS

THE MAGIC OF SHARING WISDOM

NEW & WAXING MOON: Invite inspiration and life-changing ideas to flow into your life
FULL MOON: Set an intention to make positive change or work for a humanitarian cause
WANING & DARK MOON: Let go of outdated ideas or beliefs that no longer serve you

Add sprigs of agrimony (banishing) and mint (calling in spirit and magic) to your mop water or sprinkle this concoction during a sweeping spell.

FEBRUARY

A SWEEPING SPELL
TO CHANGE THE WORLD ONE BROOM AT A TIME

Aquarius's magic is the power of the individual to influence humanity. It is the ability to detach from ideas and emotions and turn them into energy to make genuine change in the world.

ABOUT THE SPELL: An Aquarian twist on a witch's sweeping spell, you'll detach from things you take personally (when appropriate) and use those feelings for inspiration and change.

PREPARE: It's best to use a ceremonial broom or besom, but you can simply wave your hands in a sweeping motion or tie up a bundle of herbs. It would be ideal to do this spell on a windy day. However, any day is a good day for radical change.

PERFORM THE SPELL: Think of your strongest feelings like anger or injustice. Then detach from those feelings by imagining an exciting solution. Feel a paradigm-shattering view of humanity that shifts these feelings. You aren't forcing this energy outwards; you are simply offering it.

If it's hard for you to "detach" or shift your feelings when needed—here's a trick. Take a moment and focus on the space outside of yourself. First focus on your skin, then one inch outside, then farther out till you feel yourself as a part of the Earth and universe.

SWEEP OUT: Broom in hand, spiral out from the center—counterclockwise—as you sweep your inspired ideas out to the world.

SWEEP IN: Keeping an open mind is an important part of change and spiritual evolution. Invite inspiration inwards by spiraling clockwise from the edge of the space to the center.

AFTER THE SPELL: Write any new thoughts, clues, coincidences, or ideas that come to you.

Tie ribbons or feathers
to a tree and send your
prayers on the wind

Burn Frankincense and
Myrrh on holy-days to raise
the vibration on Earth

Brigid's Abbey at Kildare

IMBOLC

BRIGID'S FEAST
RITUALS TO VENERATE THE FIERY GODDESS

Keeping faith in anticipation of the coming spring is a potent theme for Imbolc, a festival which celebrates the emergence from winter's darkness into the light of the sun.

Brigid, a Celtic goddess turned Catholic Saint, is the star of many Imbolc traditions. Brigid was a nurturer, "giver," and advocate for those in need. Her miracles and magic show us that there is always enough to go around, and if you are in need—to ask for and accept help.

CRAFT A BRIGID DOLL AND ALTAR: Ancient Celts crafted dolls of Brigid to use in their Imbolc rituals. You can do the same by crafting a simple doll out of straw, sticks, herbs, or cloth. Decorate your doll with shells, ribbons, or flowers of the season to represent the coming spring. Place your doll on your altar or as the centerpiece of

your Imbolc dinner table. When the night is over, put Brigid "to bed," and she'll bring blessings to your home as you sleep.

TAKE A PILGRIMAGE TO BRIGID'S WELL:

If you can't pilgrimage to the "real" well of Brigid in Kildare, Ireland (there are actually several holy wells dedicated to her), you can visit a body of water near you for a ritual in her name.

On Imbolc eve, walk to a spring or body of water. Bring your Brigid doll, if you've made one, and a small jar or flask to collect a bit of water.

Sit in darkness for a few moments and ask Brigid for what you need. Don't be shy! Ask! Then collect a bit of water and set it on your altar.

When you feel Brigid's blessings manifesting in your life, thank her with sincere gratitude and by giving back to your community or helping others.

FEBRUARY 2022

	SUNDAY	MONDAY	TUESDAY
			*Imbolc (Fixed Date) **1** New Moon ● ≈
	30	**31**	
			8 First Quarter ◐
	6	**7**	
			15
	13	**14**	
			22
	20	**21**	
	27	**28**	**1**

WEDNESDAY	THURSDAY	FRIDAY	SATURDAY
2	Mercury Retrograde Ends ★ Imbolc 3:37 PM EST 3	4	5
9	10	11	12
16 Full Moon ○ ♌	17	☉ Sun enters Pisces ♓ 18	19
23 Last Quarter ◑	24	25	26
2 New Moon ● ♓	3	4	5

FEBRUARY 2022

MONDAY, FEBRUARY 7

TUESDAY, FEBRUARY 8
First Quarter ◑ 8:50 AM EST
► Moon void-of-course begins 11:48 PM EST

WEDNESDAY, FEBRUARY 9
Moon enters Gemini ♊ 5:28 AM EST

THURSDAY, FEBRUARY 10

FRIDAY, FEBRUARY 11
► Moon void-of-course begins 3:23 AM EST
Moon enters Cancer ♋ 6:26 PM EST

SATURDAY, FEBRUARY 12

SUNDAY, FEBRUARY 13

- The Waterbearer -
Scatter elder leaves or flowers
to the wind along with your
wishes for the world

Aquarius & Uranus
SHARING WISDOM & MAKING CHANGE

FEBRUARY 2022

MONDAY, FEBRUARY 14
► Moon void-of-course begins 5:27 AM EST
Moon enters Leo ♌ 6:17 AM EST

TUESDAY, FEBRUARY 15

WEDNESDAY, FEBRUARY 16
Full Moon ○ in Leo ♌ 11:56 AM EST
► Moon void-of-course begins 11:56 AM EST
Moon enters Virgo ♍ 3:41 PM EST

THURSDAY, FEBRUARY 17

FRIDAY, FEBRUARY 18
☉ Sun enters Pisces ♓ 11:42 AM EST
► Moon void-of-course begins 6:19 PM EST
Moon enters Libra ♎ 10:50 PM EST

SATURDAY, FEBRUARY 19

SUNDAY, FEBRUARY 20

PEACOCK
How can I embrace
my unique spirit?

ALUMINUM
- Invisibility -
How can I detach
from the undue
influence of others?

AQUAMARINE
How can I challenge
my intellect and
responsibility?

FEBRUARY 2022

MONDAY, FEBRUARY 21
▶ Moon void-of-course begins 12:02 AM EST
Moon enters Scorpio ♏ 4:17 AM EST

TUESDAY, FEBRUARY 22

WEDNESDAY, FEBRUARY 23
▶ Moon void-of-course begins 4:24 AM EST
Moon enters Sagittarius ♐ 8:27 AM EST
Last Quarter ☽ 5:32 PM EST

THURSDAY, FEBRUARY 24
▶ Moon void-of-course begins 10:24 PM EST

Lapis Lazuli
Spiritual Journey
& Connection

FRIDAY, FEBRUARY 25
Moon enters Capricorn ♑ 11:26 AM EST

SATURDAY, FEBRUARY 26

SUNDAY, FEBRUARY 27
▶ Moon void-of-course begins 9:49 AM EST
Moon enters Aquarius ♒ 1:36 PM EST

Eight Pointed Star
The Divine Order of the Universe

FEBRUARY/MARCH 2022

MONDAY, FEBRUARY 28
► Moon void-of-course begins 9:01 PM EST

TUESDAY, MARCH 1
Moon enters Pisces ♓ 3:54 PM EST

WEDNESDAY, MARCH 2
New Moon ● in Pisces ♓ 12:35 PM EST

THURSDAY, MARCH 3
► Moon void-of-course begins 4:45 PM EST
Moon enters Aries ♈ 7:53 PM EST

FRIDAY, MARCH 4

SATURDAY, MARCH 5
► Moon void-of-course begins 11:02 PM EST

SUNDAY, MARCH 6
Moon enters Taurus ♉ 3:00 AM EST

Honor Inanna with an offering of wine and incense of cedar, cypress, and juniper

- Rod & Ring -
The Earthly Plane and the Divine

INANNA
SUMERIAN GODDESS OF LOVE AND WAR

Pisces's Bag of Tricks

EMOTIONAL INTELLIGENCE
*Hold a moonstone to your
heart to connect to your intuition
and calm your emotions*

NEPTUNE
*Meditate at the water's
edge and ask for the
wisdom of the deep*

SPIRITUALITY
*Refresh and enliven your spirit
by drinking jasmine tea or adding
jasmine flowers to your bath*

PEACE AND HEALING
*Burn gardenia incense or sniff fresh
flowers to uplift your energy*

Neptune - Mutable - Water - "I Believe"

Chicory
- Ease -

Water Lily
- Peace -

PISCES

THE MAGIC OF EMOTIONS

NEW & WAXING MOON: Explore how and where you can give or receive more kindness
FULL MOON: Channel your intuitive powers to clearly see your dreams and visions
WANING & DARK MOON: Take refuge in your sacred space to recharge and go within

Burn or diffuse eucalyptus to clarify and release your emotions

Mix sea salts with crushed ash leaves and orange blossoms for a spiritually recharging bath or blessing water

MARCH

BATH OF PROPHECIES
A SEA SALT SPELL TO CHANNEL YOUR INNER GUIDE

While our Aquarius spell focused on detaching from feelings—Pisces swims the other way. Pisces is all about "the feels." The magic of Pisces is the ability to tune into emotions, intuition, and the guiding voice deep inside your soul.

ABOUT THE SPELL: We'll use Pisces magic to create a sea salt "Prophecy Powder." Use it as a bath salt or shower scrub, or to sprinkle on your tarot cards, spirit board, or other divination tool. We'll also make a delicious savory version that you can use for divinatory purposes in your cooking or kitchen spells.

PREPARE YOUR PROPHECY SALTS: Mix 1/2 cup of quality sea salt and about 1/4 cup of dried herbs and petals (mugwort, jasmine, rose, and lavender are excellent herbs for visions). If you'd prefer a shower scrub, blend the herbs and salt with 1/2 cup of jojoba oil to create a paste.

Then cast a mystical bath environment with incense, candles, dim lighting, or whatever you desire. Sprinkle the bath salts into the hot water and submerge yourself. Allow your mind to drift to nothingness as you imagine yourself in the space between worlds. Then call a prophecy to appear to you from the celestial void. For the next several days, take note of any dreams, prophecies, or visions that come to you.

KITCHEN PROPHECIES: As an alternative to the bath spell, mix Celtic sea salt with dried bay, basil, and fennel seeds. Add chili powder for an extra kick. Keep it on your table and pull some tarot cards while you're in the kitchen—or sprinkle it on whatever you've got cooking—then divine for messages in the steam.

Anoint candles
with rose and
orange oil

Eggs & Tulips
New life, creation,
and abundance

OSTARA

ROD · LADA · BABA YAGA · MAKOSH · PERUN

Celebrating Spring
Ancient Crafts for Abundant Blessings

Ostara or the spring equinox holds the most powerful seasonal energy to start new projects and phases in life. So... who do you want to be? As a witch, you get to decide. While the ancient theme of the equinox is fertility, you can use this energy to "grow" whatever you want in life.

OSTARA EGGS: Ancient Persian cultures began the tradition of painting eggs thousands of years ago. Paint real eggs, paper eggs, or wooden ones.

Use Persian Nowruz inspired designs or try Slavic Pysanka eggs painted with wax and color.

GOD POLES: Perhaps you'd prefer to carve a wooden deity statue, sometimes called a "god pole." (Clay would work, too). Procure a balsa or basswood carving block. Carefully carve the image of your deity or guide.

PREPARE: A few days or weeks before the

equinox, think deeply about who you want to be in this next cycle of life. Then write it down. (Dedicated! Studious! Loving! Confident! Aligned!)

Craft your eggs or god poles ahead of time to use as ritual tools and altar items, or work the crafting process into your ritual if you prefer.

PERFORM THE RITUAL: Set up a meditative, magical space on the day or night of the equinox.

There are no specifics here, other than to IMAGINE or FEEL your ideal life or whatever it is you desire to be. Feel it through your third eye and immerse yourself in the feeling of already having it. Spend a few minutes to deepen the sensation, then bring the feeling to the lower back of your head. If your neck gets tingly—awesome.

Challenge yourself to stay inspired for the entire day or longer.

MARCH 2022

Plant seeds on Ostara to represent what you want to manifest

	SUNDAY	MONDAY	TUESDAY
	27	28	1
	6	7	8
	13	14	15
	20 ✳ Ostara (Spring Equinox) ☉ Sun enters Aries ♈	21	22
	27	28	29

WEDNESDAY	THURSDAY	FRIDAY	SATURDAY
2 New Moon ● ♓	3	4	5
9	10 First Quarter ◐	11	12
16	17	18 Full Moon ○ ♍	19
23	24	25 Last Quarter ◑	26
30	31	1 New Moon ● ♈	2

MARCH 2022

MONDAY, MARCH 7

TUESDAY, MARCH 8
► Moon void-of-course begins 9:35 AM EST
Moon enters Gemini ♊ 1:41 PM EST

WEDNESDAY, MARCH 9

THURSDAY, MARCH 10
First Quarter ◑ 5:45 AM EST
► Moon void-of-course begins 11:43 AM EST

FRIDAY, MARCH 11
Moon enters Cancer ♋ 2:23 AM EST

SATURDAY, MARCH 12

SUNDAY, MARCH 13
► Moon void-of-course begins 11:44 AM EDT
Moon enters Leo ♌ 3:32 PM EDT

- Whale -
Resurrection
& Rebirth

Pisces & Neptune
AWARENESS OF DREAMS AND EMOTIONS
Listen to whale songs and give yourself permission to dream "big"

MARCH 2022

MONDAY, MARCH 14

TUESDAY, MARCH 15
▸ Moon void-of-course begins 6:56 AM EDT

WEDNESDAY, MARCH 16
Moon enters Virgo ♍ 12:56 AM EDT

THURSDAY, MARCH 17

FRIDAY, MARCH 18
Full Moon ○ in Virgo ♍ 3:18 AM EDT
▸ Moon void-of-course begins 4:11 AM EDT
Moon enters Libra ♎ 7:26 AM EDT

SATURDAY, MARCH 19

SUNDAY, MARCH 20
▸ Moon void-of-course begins 8:40 AM EDT
★ Ostara (Spring Equinox) 11:33 AM EDT
☉ Sun enters Aries ♈ 11:33 AM EDT
Moon enters Scorpio ♏ 11:45 AM EDT

CHAROITE
What does it feel
like to trust myself?

TIN
How can I "tinker"
to create prosperity
and allow myself to
have good things?

- Lavender -
Peace Within

CELESTITE
What does my
divine guidance
want me to know?

MARCH 2022

MONDAY, MARCH 21

TUESDAY, MARCH 22
▸ Moon void-of-course begins 12:01 PM EDT
Moon enters Sagittarius ♐ 2:58 PM EDT

WEDNESDAY, MARCH 23

THURSDAY, MARCH 24
▸ Moon void-of-course begins 8:59 AM EDT
Moon enters Capricorn ♑ 5:54 PM EDT

FRIDAY, MARCH 25
Last Quarter ◐ 1:37 AM EDT

SATURDAY, MARCH 26
▸ Moon void-of-course begins 7:51 PM EDT
Moon enters Aquarius ♒ 8:55 PM EDT

SUNDAY, MARCH 27

*Hare & Chicks
New Life*

*Dandelion Root Tea
Manifesting through
Intuition*

MARCH/APRIL 2022

MONDAY, MARCH 28
► Moon void-of-course begins 10:11 AM EDT

TUESDAY, MARCH 29
Moon enters Pisces ♓ 12:33 AM EDT

WEDNESDAY, MARCH 30

THURSDAY, MARCH 31
► Moon void-of-course begins 2:37 AM EDT
Moon enters Aries ♈ 5:30 AM EDT

FRIDAY, APRIL 1
New Moon ● in Aries ♈ 2:24 AM EDT

SATURDAY, APRIL 2
► Moon void-of-course begins 9:51 AM EDT
Moon enters Taurus ♉ 12:50 PM EDT

SUNDAY, APRIL 3

ĒOSTRE
GERMANIC GODDESS OF SPRING

INTUITION | REFLECTION | INTENTIONS | IMPORTANT THINGS | GOALS

Aries's Bag of Tricks
Confidence
Burn red or orange candles to stoke your inner fire
Courage
Carry a ruby or rub dragon's blood resin on the soles of your shoes
MATCHES FROM mars
Personal Power
Make a blackthorn wand to manifest your wishes

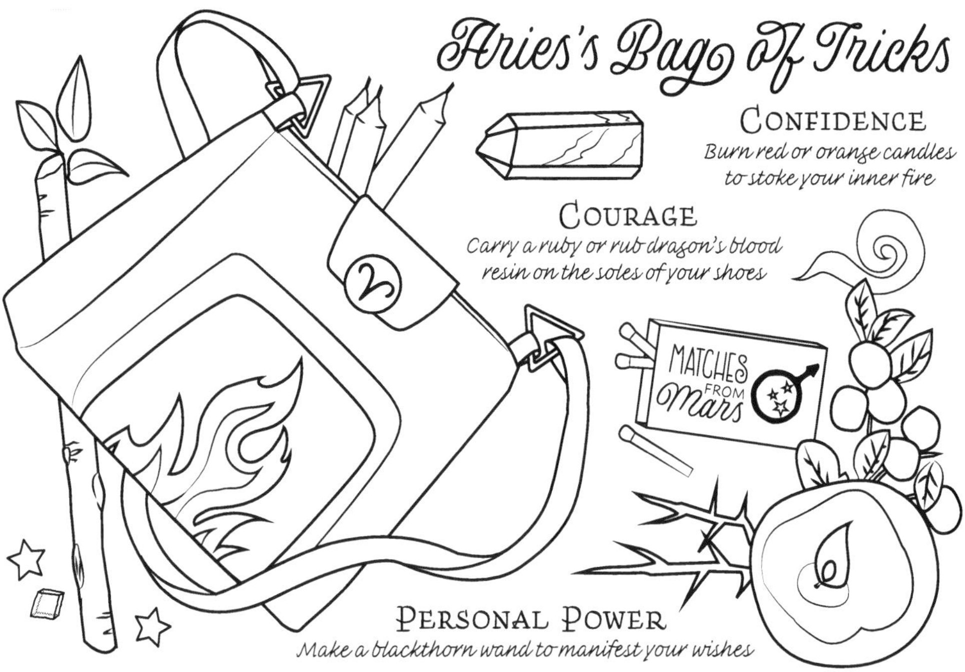

The Ram
Tenacity

Mars - Cardinal - Fire - "I Am"

Hawthorn
Witch Power

ARIES

THE MAGIC OF ACTION & WILL

NEW & WAXING MOON: Start new projects that ignite your passions and curiosities
FULL MOON: Empower yourself to set meaningful goals and commit to following through
WANING & DARK MOON: Take time to blow off steam in nature or explore new activities

If you see Mars on Tuesday commit to taking action towards your desires

Stargaze on the dark moon. Drink wormwood tea or burn it as incense to summon spirits—including your own.

APRIL

The Fire Within
Spells to Raise the Energy of Your Spirit

You've set your spring equinox intentions into the universe, now sit back and wait for them to appear, right?! Yes! Err... No, not quite. You've got to take some "inspired action." The spring equinox begins the transit of the sun in Aries, and Aries season is an auspicious time for action.

The magic of Aries is enthusiasm and energy of beginnings. In this spell, you'll channel that eager spirit and inspire yourself to do what you wish.

PREPARE: Think back to your Capricorn spell and your Ostara intentions. What bold step do you need to take that you haven't yet? It's probably that thing that excites the heck out of you but also scares you a little (or a lot). It could be small-ish (a new haircut or art class) or bigger (moving house, a new career, etc). Figure it out and write it down. Then try one of these spells to

help you take that magical step forward.

CANDLES: Prepare several small spell candles with herbs and oils that represent strength and courage. Perhaps a white, red, or orange candle with clove oil and dragon's blood resin. Tie the candles into a bundle with red string, then burn one whenever you need a bit of "Aries" magic.

TEA: Make a special blend of green tea with ginger and ginseng. Brew yourself a cup and then take that bold step you've been wanting to take.

SEEDS OF STRENGTH: If you like snacks, roast pumpkin or sunflower seeds with cumin, coriander, salt, and jalapeño. Store the seeds in jars tied with red string, then eat 'em whenever you need to enliven your spirit.

A SHOE SPELL: Rub a drop of musk or cedar oil in your shoes for a magical boost of fiery courage.

APRIL 2022

A Black Moon (second dark moon in a month) occurs on April 30, 2022. Set an intention to change a habit or bring something out of the deepest shadows.

SUNDAY	MONDAY	TUESDAY
27	28	29
3	4	5
10	11	12
17	18	19 ☉ Sun enters Taurus ♉
24	25	26

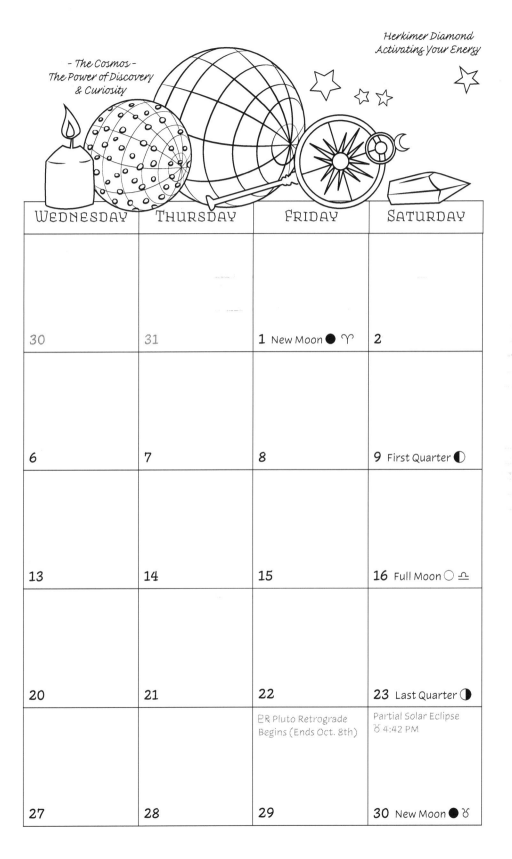

- The Cosmos -
The Power of Discovery
& Curiosity

Herkimer Diamond
Activating Your Energy

WEDNESDAY	THURSDAY	FRIDAY	SATURDAY
30	31	1 New Moon ● ♈	2
6	7	8	9 First Quarter ◐
13	14	15	16 Full Moon ○ ♎
20	21	22	23 Last Quarter ◑
27	28	29 ℞ Pluto Retrograde Begins (Ends Oct. 8th)	30 New Moon ● ♉ Partial Solar Eclipse ♉ 4:42 PM

APRIL 2022

MONDAY, APRIL 4
▸ Moon void-of-course begins 9:53 PM EDT
Moon enters Gemini ♊ 11:05 PM EDT

TUESDAY, APRIL 5

WEDNESDAY, APRIL 6
▸ Moon void-of-course begins 11:15 PM EDT

THURSDAY, APRIL 7
Moon enters Cancer ♋ 11:30 AM EDT

FRIDAY, APRIL 8

SATURDAY, APRIL 9
First Quarter ◑ 2:48 AM EDT
▸ Moon void-of-course begins 9:01 PM EDT

SUNDAY, APRIL 10
Moon enters Leo ♌ 12:00 AM EDT

Iron Meteorites & the Power of the Cosmos

Aries & Mars
ACTION, COURAGE, AND PASSION
Place iron nails in a jar of water when Mars is visible.
Let the nails rust, then use the water for elemental power.

APRIL 2022

MONDAY, APRIL 11

TUESDAY, APRIL 12
▸ Moon void-of-course begins 6:16 AM EDT
Moon enters Virgo ♍ 10:07 AM EDT

WEDNESDAY, APRIL 13

THURSDAY, APRIL 14
▸ Moon void-of-course begins 2:11 PM EDT
Moon enters Libra ♎ 4:46 PM EDT

FRIDAY, APRIL 15

SATURDAY, APRIL 16
Full Moon ○ in Libra ♎ 2:55 PM EDT
▸ Moon void-of-course begins 5:57 PM EDT
Moon enters Scorpio ♏ 8:22 PM EDT

SUNDAY, APRIL 17

Cumin
How can I protect my spirit from the evil eye?

Cinnamon
How can I raise my vibration?

Garnish your snacks with nasturtiums, wild mustard, & spicy greens

Chiles
How can I maximize my energy?

APRIL 2022

MONDAY, APRIL 18
► Moon void-of-course begins 7:55 PM EDT
Moon enters Sagittarius ♐ 10:16 PM EDT

TUESDAY, APRIL 19
☉ Sun enters Taurus ♉ 10:24 PM EDT

WEDNESDAY, APRIL 20
► Moon void-of-course begins 4:56 PM EDT
Moon enters Capricorn ♑ 11:53 PM EDT

THURSDAY, APRIL 21

FRIDAY, APRIL 22
► Moon void-of-course begins 11:53 PM EDT

SATURDAY, APRIL 23
Moon enters Aquarius ♒ 2:19 AM EDT
Last Quarter ◗ 7:56 AM EDT

SUNDAY, APRIL 24
► Moon void-of-course begins 8:33 PM EDT

Toadflax

Oak

Bay

Mullein

FIRE
THE ELEMENT OF PASSION

APRIL/MAY 2022

MONDAY, APRIL 25
Moon enters Pisces ♓ 6:15 AM EDT

TUESDAY, APRIL 26

WEDNESDAY, APRIL 27
➤ Moon void-of-course begins 9:37 AM EDT
Moon enters Aries ♈ 12:10 PM EDT

THURSDAY, APRIL 28

FRIDAY, APRIL 29
♇℞ Pluto Retrograde begins 2:36 PM EDT - Oct. 8th
➤ Moon void-of-course begins 5:38 PM EDT
Moon enters Taurus ♉ 8:19 PM EDT

SATURDAY, APRIL 30
New Moon ● in Taurus ♉ 4:28 PM EDT
Partial Solar Eclipse in Taurus ♉ 4:42 PM

SUNDAY, MAY 1
★ Beltane (Fixed Festival Date)

FIRE WITCHERY

- Work with candles and flames.
- Eat spicy foods or do things that make you sweaty or hot.
- Meditate facing south and imagine the sun's heat filling you with energy.
- Repeat a mantra like, "I am alive!"
- Burn a fiery incense like rose geranium and sweet woodruff to summon your courage and drive.
- Do things you're passionate about.

Taurus's Bag of Tricks

DEPENDABLE
Feel the abundance of the
Earth by eating grains like
oats and barley

EARTHLY PLEASURES
Bake a strawberry rhubarb
pie or enjoy a fruity treat

- Love -
Rose Quartz &
Daisies

VENUS'S BEAUTY
Decorate or find
creative inspiration in
natural materials

SLOW & STEADY
Wear an emerald to
increase your patience

Cows
Dependability

Venus - Fixed - Earth - "I Have"

Foxglove
Peace At Home

Malachite
Grounding

TAURUS

THE MAGIC OF FEELING GROUNDED

NEW & WAXING MOON: Create routines of self-care or enhance your style and decor
FULL MOON: Celebrate and enjoy pleasurable experiences that engage your senses
WANING & DARK MOON: Work in the garden and finish up what's on your to-do list

Find the first spring daisy and possess a delightful "spirit of coquetry"

Stop what you're doing and lounge on comfy pillows

The Sanctuary of Earth
Creating Sacred Space Outdoors

Taurus embodies the healing qualities of a luxurious outdoor space. It's a sign of cultivating the earth and (sustainably!) enjoying pleasurable experiences and natural treasures. Taurus helps you think from a place of comfort and a feeling of being cared for—quality fabrics, nice incense, and a new pillow every once in a while.

WITCHING IN THE GARDEN: If you've been thinking about witching up your garden or creating an outdoor sanctuary, Taurus is a lovely time to do it. And it doesn't have to be outdoors, one small low-light houseplant or a couple of herbs is enough indoor garden space to make magic happen. Start by cleaning up—pulling weeds, getting rid of anything that's broken or tired, and giving yourself a blank slate.

SET THE "TAURUS" TONE: Taurus loves the beauty of natural materials. Think "quality over quantity." For example, take your time thrifting for one perfect altar table or plant stand instead of trying to accomplish too much at once and using multitudinous lower-quality items.

NO PLANTS NECESSARY: Are you a green witch without a green thumb? No worries! Try a rock garden or a small altar with a couple of beautiful statues. A stone circle or labyrinth will make a big impact on the spirit of your space, even if you don't plant anything green around it.

CONSECRATE THE SPACE: After you've cleared and set your space, have a candlelight procession or ceremony at any time you see fit. Burn floral or earthy scents like vanilla or eucalyptus. Dedicate yourself to tend to the Earth's well-being as it cares for you.

- Magic Knot -
The Power of the
Elements

Cast mugwort and violets into
your Beltane fire while you make a
wish for something wonderful

BELTANE

WEAVING THE MAYPOLE
AND THE RITUALS OF SPRING

The most iconic image of May Day or Beltane is the maypole. You might envision idyllic scenes of robed children dancing merrily with flower crowns or a coven of voluptuous nude witches.

Weaving the maypole symbolizes the coming together of the seasons and elements to create life on Earth. In archaic Roman practices, the maypole ribbons represented protection. Witches still use ribbons in this manner today, as a way to send wishes and prayers "on the wind."

MAYPOLE MAGIC: While most do not have the space, equipment, and coven to do a full-on maypole dance, if you do—by all means—do it! However, if you are practicing as a solitary witch or just want to celebrate on a smaller scale—there are plenty of things you can do.

MINI MAYPOLE: Create an altar-sized version of a maypole and weave it together on May Eve. Use a wooden dowel and an even number of ribbons attached to the top with a pushpin. (Six ribbons will do, but you can use more). Secure a crown of flowers or greenery on top, then stand the pole in a jar filled with sand.

FAERIE POPPETS: Faerie magic is powerful on Beltane. Make a tiny braided faerie doll out of wheat, corn, straw, ribbons, or strips of fabric. Give it wings to fly, then hang it out in a tree to let the faeries know they're welcome.

WOVEN MAGIC: Make friendship bracelets or lanyards with embroidery thread and cording. Things you make for others will be extra special.

Or use this powerful season to craft a tool for your magical practice, like a cingulum (magical belt), woven altar cloth, or pendulum cord.

MAY 2022

	SUNDAY	MONDAY	TUESDAY
	★ Beltane (Fixed Date) 1	2	3
	8 First Quarter ◐	9	Mercury Retrograde Begins (Ends June 3rd) 10
	15	Total Lunar Eclipse in Scorpio ♏ 12:11 AM 16 Full Moon ○ ♏	17
	22 Last Quarter ◑	23	24
	29	30 New Moon ● ♊	31

WEDNESDAY	THURSDAY	FRIDAY	SATURDAY
4	★ Beltane 8:25 AM EDT 5	6	7
11	12	13	14
18	19	☉ Sun enters Gemini ♊ 20	21
25	26	27	28
1	2	Mercury Retrograde Ends 4:00 AM EDT 3	Saturn Retrograde Begins (Ends Oct. 23rd) 4

MAY 2022

MONDAY, MAY 2
▶ Moon void-of-course begins 6:13 AM EDT
Moon enters Gemini ♊ 6:49 AM EDT

TUESDAY, MAY 3

WEDNESDAY, MAY 4
▶ Moon void-of-course begins 4:37 PM EDT
Moon enters Cancer ♋ 7:05 PM EDT

THURSDAY, MAY 5
★ Beltane (Astronomical Date) 8:25 AM EST

FRIDAY, MAY 6

SATURDAY, MAY 7
▶ Moon void-of-course begins 6:25 AM EDT
Moon enters Leo ♌ 7:50 AM EDT

SUNDAY, MAY 8
First Quarter ◑ 8:21 PM EDT

- Copper -
Natural Beauty
& Earth's Wisdom

Scry into a
copper bowl on
Friday

Green Calcite
Abundance

Taurus & Venus
ENJOYING LIFE

MAY 2022

LYRE
Celestial Harmony
Pull seven tarot cards for clues on
how to bring harmony into your life

MONDAY, MAY 9
► Moon void-of-course begins 8:38 AM EDT
Moon enters Virgo ♍ 6:52 PM EDT

TUESDAY, MAY 10
☿℞ Mercury Retrograde begins 7:47 AM EDT - June 3rd

WEDNESDAY, MAY 11
► Moon void-of-course begins 11:59 PM EDT

*Cow
What is best solved
by staying put?*

THURSDAY, MAY 12
Moon enters Libra ♎ 2:30 AM EDT

FRIDAY, MAY 13

COPPER
How can I make
use of the
resources I have?

SATURDAY, MAY 14
► Moon void-of-course begins 4:07 AM EDT
Moon enters Scorpio ♏ 6:34 AM EDT

COLUMBINE
What will bring me
more love and
happiness in life?

SUNDAY, MAY 15

MAY 2022

MONDAY, MAY 16
Total Lunar Eclipse in Scorpio ♏ 12:11 AM
Full Moon ○ in Scorpio ♏ 12:14 AM EDT
► Moon void-of-course begins 5:28 AM EDT
Moon enters Sagittarius ♐ 7:48 AM EDT

TUESDAY, MAY 17
► Moon void-of-course begins 11:59 PM EDT

WEDNESDAY, MAY 18
Moon enters Capricorn ♑ 8:03 AM EDT

THURSDAY, MAY 19

FRIDAY, MAY 20
► Moon void-of-course begins 7:59 AM EDT
Moon enters Aquarius ♒ 8:53 AM EDT
☉ Sun enters Gemini ♊ 9:22 PM EDT

SATURDAY, MAY 21

SUNDAY, MAY 22
► Moon void-of-course begins 3:19 AM EDT
Moon enters Pisces ♓ 11:49 AM EDT
Last Quarter ◑ 2:43 PM EDT

Craft a Cernunnos poppet and stuff it with cedar, vetivert, and juniper berries

Place a piece of quartz inside before sewing it up, and anoint with a drop of amber oil

MAY 2022

MONDAY, MAY 23

TUESDAY, MAY 24
► Moon void-of-course 5:33 PM EDT
Moon enters Aries ♈ 5:39 PM EDT

WEDNESDAY, MAY 25

THURSDAY, MAY 26
► Moon void-of-course begins 11:20 PM EDT

FRIDAY, MAY 27
Moon enters Taurus ♉ 2:22 AM EDT

SATURDAY, MAY 28

SUNDAY, MAY 29
► Moon void-of-course begins 10:11 AM EDT
Moon enters Gemini ♊ 1:24 PM EDT

*Help protect animals
and wildlands to
honor Cernunnos*

CERNUNNOS
CELTIC GOD OF THE WILDERNESS

MAY/JUNE 2022

MONDAY, MAY 30
New Moon ● in Gemini ♊ 7:30 AM EDT

TUESDAY, MAY 31
► Moon void-of-course begins 4:10 PM EDT

WEDNESDAY, JUNE 1
Moon enters Cancer ♋ 1:49 AM EDT

THURSDAY, JUNE 2

FRIDAY, JUNE 3
☿ ℞ Mercury Retrograde ends 4:00 AM EDT
► Moon void-of-course begins 11:15 AM EDT
Moon enters Leo ♌ 2:37 PM EDT

SATURDAY, JUNE 4
♄ ℞ Saturn Retrograde 5:47 PM EDT - Oct. 23rd

SUNDAY, JUNE 5
► Moon void-of-course begins 7:12 PM EDT

Honor Gaia by tending to the Earth, feeding animals and insects, or by leaving an offering of fruit, honey, or a special crystal buried deep in the ground.

- Flower of Life -
The Power and Patterns
of the Cosmos

GAIA
GREEK GODDESS OF THE EARTH

Gemini's Bag Of Tricks

ACTIVITY
Make a hazel wand or charm bag stuffed with dried ferns to lead you on adventures

VOICE
Speak!

Shawm & Woodwinds

RELATIONSHIPS
Burn benzoin incense to "clear the air" and enhance magical conversation

MERCURY
The power of your mind

CURIOSITY
Sniff fresh lavender while reading to relax and open your mind

GEMINI

THE MAGIC OF COMMUNICATION

NEW & WAXING MOON: Talk to new people and follow your curiosity to explore new things
FULL MOON: Use your voice and communication skills to speak up and empower others
WANING & DARK MOON: Take time to rest, recuperate, and recharge with friends or family

Mix crystal-infused or moon-charged water with your watercolor paints

JUNE

BREAKING YOUR HEX
UNSPEAK THE CURSES YOU'VE CURSED ON YOURSELF

Gemini's magic lies in communication and the duality of talking and listening—the dark and light behind words and the two sides of a conversation.

Most of the curses or "dark" magic thrown at you comes from... you! Yes! We often curse ourselves unwittingly. The good news is you can undo these pesky curses with a bit of magic.

Color and sound are both "airy" magical mechanisms. In this spell, you'll use color, sound, and the magic of Gemini to break a few hexes.

THE COLOR OF YOUR CURSES: Close your eyes and feel the color of the curse. Then write the curse in that color. Find the opposite "hex-breaker" color on the color wheel and write your hex-breaker in the opposite color. Example:

(In yellow): I'm not good enough to _____.

(In purple): I am powerful and I am ready for this!

THE SOUND OF YOUR CURSES: Distill each curse you've identified to one word, random sound, or phrase. Then find the opposite "hex-breaker" sound (pick the first thing to your mind).

Say the curse slowly: *Insecurity.* How does it feel? Does your chest slump? Your heart ache?

Then say the hex-breaker: *Confidence.* Does your energy rise somewhere? How does that feel?

NEUTRALIZE THE CURSES: Once you've tuned into these subtle vibrations of sound and color, work with the energy to break the curses. Break a yellow curse of insecurity by wearing purple and speaking mantras about trusting yourself, or work with purple crystals or purple candles. Go one step further and identify which chakra this curse might relate to, then work with that chakra until you feel the energy shift.

Harvest herbs on midsummer to imbue them with extra magic

- Hurdy-Gurdy -
Multiple sounds at once and the power of air

LITHA

Ring bells and play horns at dawn to welcome the sun

Find the first white lily of the season and make a wish for strength

RECEIVING WITH GRACE
AND THE MAGIC OF LITHA'S BRIGHT LIGHT

The light of abundance and blessings of the sun are always shining on you—but are you allowing yourself to receive them?

Midsummer, or Litha, marks the longest day of the year and is the celebration of the sun's full strength. The full sun at Litha allows us to see many things we normally can't or don't want to see, like turning on a bright light and suddenly realizing there's dust everywhere.

The darkest shadows also fall from the brightest lights—a powerful duality.

One of the common personal "shadows" you might uncover in yourself is resistance to receiving. You may want or need something, but when it comes time to receive it—perhaps you freak out and step back because of guilt, insecurity, or fear of your own success.

The full light of Litha is a powerful time to allow the abundance of light and the empowerment of your most vibrant self.

The magic is in allowing—but does that feel hard? Do you want to work for it or petition your deity on your knees in an elaborate ritual before you can have your blessings?

PREPARE: Pick flowers ethically or buy a small bouquet from a local farm or seller. Create a mandala (circular pattern) with the flowers and tea lights, leaving room to place a deck of tarot cards or a small notebook in the middle.

Light the candles, then pull three tarot cards to "shine a light" on how you can easily receive what you need in abundance. Alternately, after the candle has shone on the notebook, free-write on its pages and allow your subconscious to tell you the same.

JUNE 2022

SUNDAY	MONDAY	TUESDAY
29	30 New Moon ● ♊	31
5	6	7 First Quarter ◑
12	13	14 Full Moon ○ ♐
19	20 Last Quarter ◑	21 ★ Litha (Summer Solstice) ⊙ Sun enters Cancer ♋
26	27	28 New Moon ● ♋ Neptune Retrograde Begins (Ends Dec. 3rd)

Place a double-terminated crystal on your altar to enhance the flow of energy

St. John's Wort
Happiness

WEDNESDAY	THURSDAY	FRIDAY	SATURDAY
		Mercury Retrograde Ends 4:00 AM EDT	Saturn Retrograde Begins (Ends Oct. 23rd)
1	2	3	4
8	9	10	11
15	16	17	18
22	23	24	25
29	30	1	2

JUNE 2022

MONDAY, JUNE 6
Moon enters Virgo ♍ 2:22 AM EDT

TUESDAY, JUNE 7
First Quarter ◐ 10:48 AM EDT

WEDNESDAY, JUNE 8
► Moon void-of-course begins 8:09 AM EDT
Moon enters Libra ♎ 11:23 AM EDT

THURSDAY, JUNE 9

FRIDAY, JUNE 10
► Moon void-of-course begins 1:36 PM EDT
Moon enters Scorpio ♏ 4:41 PM EDT

SATURDAY, JUNE 11

SUNDAY, JUNE 12
► Moon void-of-course begins 5:40 PM EDT
Moon enters Sagittarius ♐ 6:30 PM EDT

LILY
OF THE VALLEY

How can I raise
my spirits and
uplift others?

ALMOND
WOOD
What treasures
await if I follow
my curiosity?

Gemini & Mercury
CURIOUSER AND CURIOUSER

JUNE 2022

MONDAY, JUNE 13

TUESDAY, JUNE 14
Full Moon ○ in Sagittarius ♐ 7:52 AM EDT
► Moon void-of-course begins 10:58 AM EDT
Moon enters Capricorn ♑ 6:14 PM EDT

WEDNESDAY, JUNE 15

THURSDAY, JUNE 16
► Moon void-of-course begins 2:41 PM EDT
Moon enters Aquarius ♒ 5:45 PM EDT

FRIDAY, JUNE 17

SATURDAY, JUNE 18
► Moon void-of-course begins 2:50 PM EDT
Moon enters Pisces ♓ 7:02 PM EDT

SUNDAY, JUNE 19

YELLOW
AGATE

How can I embrace both the dark and light in life?

JUNE 2022

MONDAY, JUNE 20
▸ Moon void-of-course begins 11:11 PM EDT
Last Quarter ☽ 11:11 PM EDT
Moon enters Aries ♈ 11:37 PM EDT

TUESDAY, JUNE 21
★ Litha (Summer Solstice) 5:14 AM EST
☉ Sun enters Cancer ♋ 5:14 AM EDT

WEDNESDAY, JUNE 22

THURSDAY, JUNE 23
▸ Moon void-of-course begins 4:02 AM EDT
Moon enters Taurus ♉ 7:58 AM EDT

FRIDAY, JUNE 24

SATURDAY, JUNE 25
▸ Moon void-of-course begins 3:02 PM EDT
Moon enters Gemini ♊ 7:13 PM EDT

SUNDAY, JUNE 26

Chamomile

Eucalyptus
& Lilac

WATER
THE ELEMENT OF EMOTIONS

JUNE/JULY 2022

MONDAY, JUNE 27
► Moon void-of-course begins 10:38 PM EDT

TUESDAY, JUNE 28
♆℞ Neptune Retrograde 3:55 AM EDT - Dec. 3rd
Moon enters Cancer ♋ 7:53 AM EDT
New Moon ● in Cancer ♋ 10:52 PM EDT

WEDNESDAY, JUNE 29

THURSDAY, JUNE 30
► Moon void-of-course begins 4:14 PM EDT
Moon enters Leo ♌ 8:39 PM EDT

FRIDAY, JULY 1

SATURDAY, JULY 2

SUNDAY, JULY 3
► Moon void-of-course begins 5:59 AM
Moon enters Virgo ♍ 8:29 AM EDT

WATER WITCHERY

- Bless yourself in a body of water.
- Take ritual baths or swim.
- Meditate facing west and imagine yourself floating in a sea of intuition.
- Repeat a mantra like, "I know the language of my feelings."
- Bless your water before you drink it.
- Do divination or journaling and introspection to get in touch with your feelings.

Seaweed

INTUITION | REFLECTION | INTENTIONS | IMPORTANT THINGS | GOALS

Cancer's Bag of Tricks

Calming
TRANQUILITY

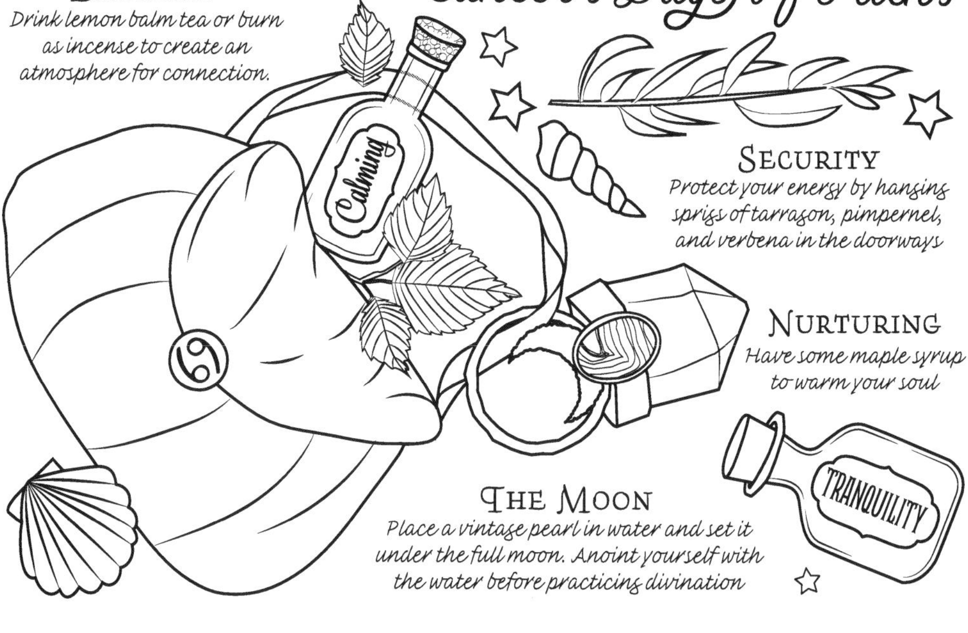

Empathy

Drink lemon balm tea or burn as incense to create an atmosphere for connection.

Security

Protect your energy by hanging sprigs of tarragon, pimpernel, and verbena in the doorways

Nurturing

Have some maple syrup to warm your soul

The Moon

Place a vintage pearl in water and set it under the full moon. Anoint yourself with the water before practicing divination

The Moon - Cardinal - Water - "I Feel"

Crab
Softness &
Strength

White Rose
The Moon

Acanthus
Immortality
of the Soul

CANCER

THE MAGIC OF SENSITIVITY

NEW & WAXING MOON: Follow your intuition and flow through life in your own way and time
FULL MOON: Listen to your heightened emotions and do cozy ritual work and spells at home
WANING & DARK MOON: Relax and recharge with familiar routines and comforting activities

Mix a relaxing bath potion with
sea salt, verbena, chamomile,
and white rose petals

A Potent Moonwater
A Spell to Turn Sensitivity Into Strength

Magic lies in the tension between strength and sensitivity, the superpower of the Cancer sign.

Sensitivity often causes us to put up protective armor, which can constrict growth.

In this spell we'll use the liminal space between these two to make some serious magic happen.

IDENTIFY YOUR ILL-FITTING CRAB SHELL

Cancer is the sign of the moon—the luminary of sensitivity to feelings, emotion, and psychic energy. Use those powers to dig deep into your hidden feelings, and ultimately find a point of sensitivity or growth that you've been avoiding.

MAKE THE MOONWATER: If you can, walk along the seashore at dawn or dusk under the moon in Cancer, until you find a shell and a small hagstone. Or substitute with sea salt or seaweed.

At the next full moon, place the shell, the hagstone, and one vintage pearl (optional) in a jar or bowl of water. Set it out under the moon at dusk, then busy yourself with cozy things at home for the evening.

Before you go to sleep, stand out under the moon and ask for the power and strength to change out of your ill-fitting crab shell.

Envision yourself waking up in the morning and knowing exactly what you need to do, then doing it easily. Imagine yourself in three months having made your changes. Feel how pleased you are with how much you've grown.

In the morning, remove the hagstone, the shell, and the pearl from the water and return them to the sea. Transfer the water to an airtight jar, and set it on your altar, or use it in spells to release blocks and constrictions.

JULY 2022

SUNDAY	MONDAY	TUESDAY
		Neptune Retrograde Begins (Ends Dec. 3rd) 28 New Moon ● ♋
26	27	
3	4	5
10	11	12
17	18	19
24	25	26
31	★ Lughnasadh (Fixed Date) 1	2

WEDNESDAY	THURSDAY	FRIDAY	SATURDAY
29	30	1	2
6 First Quarter ◑	7	8	9
13 Full Moon ○ ♋	14	15	16
20 Last Quarter ◐	21	⊙ Sun enters Leo ♌ 22	23
27	Jupiter Retrograde Begins (Ends Nov. 23rd) 28 New Moon ● ♌	29	30
3	4	5 First Quarter ◑	6

JULY 2022

MONDAY, JULY 4

TUESDAY, JULY 5
► Moon void-of-course begins 2:03 PM EDT
Moon enters Libra ♎ 6:24 PM EDT

WEDNESDAY, JULY 6
First Quarter ◐ 10:14 AM EDT

THURSDAY, JULY 7
► Moon void-of-course begins 9:04 PM EDT

FRIDAY, JULY 8
Moon enters Scorpio ♏ 1:15 AM EDT

SATURDAY, JULY 9

SUNDAY, JULY 10
► Moon void-of-course begins 12:34 AM EDT
Moon enters Sagittarius ♐ 4:34 AM EDT

Cancer & The Moon
INTUITIVE POWERS

JULY 2022

MONDAY, JULY 11
▶ Moon void-of-course begins 9:42 PM EDT

TUESDAY, JULY 12
Moon enters Capricorn ♑ 5:01 AM EDT

WEDNESDAY, JULY 13
Full Moon ○ in Capricorn ♑ 2:38 PM EDT

THURSDAY, JULY 14
▶ Moon void-of-course begins 12:17 AM EDT
Moon enters Aquarius ♒ 4:13 AM EDT

FRIDAY, JULY 15

SATURDAY, JULY 16
▶ Moon void-of-course begins 12:36 AM EDT
Moon enters Pisces ♓ 4:18 AM EDT

SUNDAY, JULY 17

MOONSTONE
What intuitive messages have I been unwilling to accept?

Pearl
Intuition

SILVER
How can I trust the power and strength of my intuition?

HIBISCUS
How can I love and care for myself on a deeper level?

Makau and Hei Matau
Strength and Safety

JULY 2022

MONDAY, JULY 18
► Moon void-of-course begins 2:43 AM EDT
Moon enters Aries ♈ 7:17 AM EDT

TUESDAY, JULY 19

WEDNESDAY, JULY 20
► Moon void-of-course begins 10:19 AM EDT
Last Quarter ◑ 10:19 AM EDT
Moon enters Taurus ♉ 2:23 PM EDT

THURSDAY, JULY 21

FRIDAY, JULY 22
☉ Sun enters Leo ♌ 4:06 PM EDT
► Moon void-of-course begins 7:45 PM EDT

SATURDAY, JULY 23
Moon enters Gemini ♊ 1:12 AM EDT

SUNDAY, JULY 24

Look for Hina on the surface of the ocean under the full moon

HINA
POLYNESIAN GODDESS OF THE MOON

JULY 2022

Make a protection charm by burying a coconut filled with herbs like aloe, seaweed, or datura

MONDAY, JULY 25
▸ Moon void-of-course begins 4:14 AM EDT
Moon enters Cancer ♋ 1:54 AM EDT

TUESDAY, JULY 26

WEDNESDAY, JULY 27
▸ Moon void-of-course begins 8:54 PM EDT

THURSDAY, JULY 28
Moon enters Leo ♌ 2:35 AM EDT
New Moon ● in Leo ♌ 1:55 PM EDT
♃℞ Jupiter Retrograde 4:38 PM EDT - Nov. 23rd

FRIDAY, JULY 29

SATURDAY, JULY 30
▸ Moon void-of-course begins 12:29 AM EDT
Moon enters Virgo ♍ 2:11 PM EDT

SUNDAY, JULY 31

Anthurium
Friendship & Pleasant
Company

Leo's Bag of Tricks

SELF-EXPRESSION
Put a ruby in your pocket while creating or socializing to encourage true expression

THE SUN
Refresh your light by bathing in sunflower petals

STRENGTH
Harness Leo's power in an oak wand consecrated with saffron oil

CHARISMA
Bundle rue and rosemary to dispel negativity and give yourself space to shine

The Sun - Fixed - Fire - "I Create"

Lion & Marigold
Strength of Heart
and Spirit

LEO

THE MAGIC OF SELF-EXPRESSION

NEW & WAXING MOON: Use creative outlets to discover new things about yourself
FULL MOON: Channel your power and strength through fire rituals and energy-raising
WANING & DARK MOON: Take time to reflect on who you are and who you want to become

Write wishes on bay leaves, then burn the leaves to make your wishes come true

Get yourself some "big hair" or big showy flowers like zinnias or dahlias

AUGUST

EMPOWERMENT OF SELF
A FIERY ALTAR TO THE DEITY WITHIN

The sun is a star that brightens up the black of the cosmos. You are also made of stars, and you have an inner light that is wholly yours to shine.

"Light" isn't about being happy or positive. It's about being true to yourself, despite what others think, even if you are vilified or stand alone.

Leo's darkest shadow is confusion about who they are when they try to please others. The simple (but not easy) solution is to be true to yourself—always. In this spell, you're going to stand in your true sense of self and roar about it with flames all around you.

CREATE AN ALTAR AND OATH: Create a fire altar to yourself, supported by your guides or deities if you like. Get yourself some new candles or a little gift, a crown, a book, a coffee cup, or some flowers. Place the gift on your altar.

Write an oath that spells out your dedication.

Example: "I, (your name,) declare myself ruler of my own life and magical realm. It is my sacred duty to protect this expression of myself. Freedom to express myself honestly is the magic that will inspire others to do the same. And so it is."

CAST YOUR SPELL: If possible, dance around a bonfire while the moon or sun (or both) is in Leo. Or use candles instead. Then ask the truest version of yourself to come to you. Feel the energy of your most empowered, brilliant self emerge through your body. Then speak your oath.

When you feel your energy rising, imagine a ball of light over your head, shining down on your shoulders, and filling you with magic.

At the peak of your energy, roar. Yes! *Do it*. Sit in your power for a moment, then feel it grounding and centering through you and into the earth.

Grow catnip to attract positive energy and strengthen the magic between you and your cats

AUGUST 2022

SUNDAY	MONDAY	TUESDAY
31	*Lughnasadh (Fixed Date) 1	2
*Lughnasadh 8:36 AM EST 7	8	9
14	15	16
21	☉ Sun enters Virgo ♍ 22	23
28	29	30

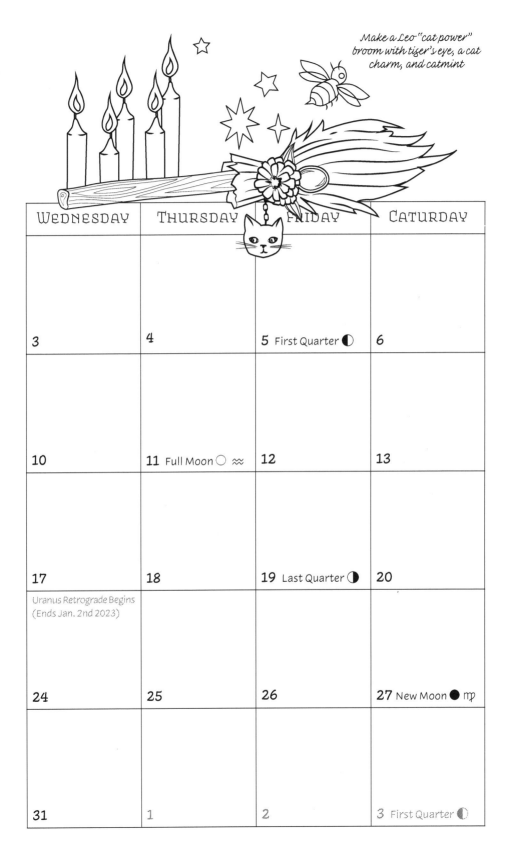

Make a Leo "cat power" broom with tiger's eye, a cat charm, and catmint

WEDNESDAY	THURSDAY	FRIDAY	CATURDAY
3	4	5 First Quarter ◗	6
10	11 Full Moon ○ ≈	12	13
17	18	19 Last Quarter ◗	20
24 Uranus Retrograde Begins (Ends Jan. 2nd 2023)	25	26	27 New Moon ● ♍
31	1	2	3 First Quarter ◗

AUGUST 2022

MONDAY, AUGUST 1
★ Lughnasadh (Fixed Festival Date)
▶ Moon void-of-course begins 6:29 PM EDT

TUESDAY, AUGUST 2
Moon enters Libra ♎ 12:04 AM EDT

WEDNESDAY, AUGUST 3

THURSDAY, AUGUST 4
▶ Moon void-of-course begins 2:19 AM EDT
Moon enters Scorpio ♏ 7:47 AM EDT

FRIDAY, AUGUST 5
First Quarter ◗ 7:06 AM EDT

SATURDAY, AUGUST 6
▶ Moon void-of-course begins 7:24 AM EDT
Moon enters Sagittarius ♐ 12:39 PM EDT

SUNDAY, AUGUST 7
★ Lughnasadh (Astronomical Date) 8:36 AM EST

Saffron
How can I use my strength to create joy?

Citrine
What energizes me to create?

Gold – the Sun
How can I shine as my brightest self?

Bay
How can I maximize my energy?

Leo & The Sun
THE POWER OF YOURSELF

AUGUST 2022

MONDAY, AUGUST 8
► Moon void-of-course begins 6:30 AM EDT
Moon enters Capricorn ♑ 2:39 PM EDT

TUESDAY, AUGUST 9

WEDNESDAY, AUGUST 10
► Moon void-of-course begins 12:39 PM EDT
Moon enters Aquarius ♒ 2:44 PM EDT

THURSDAY, AUGUST 11
Full Moon ○ in Aquarius ♒ 9:36 PM EDT

FRIDAY, AUGUST 12
► Moon void-of-course begins 7:07 AM EDT
Moon enters Pisces ♓ 2:46 PM EDT

SATURDAY, AUGUST 13

SUNDAY, AUGUST 14
► Moon void-of-course begins 11:10 AM EDT
Moon enters Aries ♈ 4:45 PM EDT

GODDESS GRANT US
Strength

*Gather your strength under
the shade of an oak tree*

AUGUST 2022

MONDAY, AUGUST 15

TUESDAY, AUGUST 16
► Moon void-of-course begins 4:18 PM EDT
Moon enters Taurus ♉ 10:24 PM EDT

WEDNESDAY, AUGUST 17

THURSDAY, AUGUST 18

FRIDAY, AUGUST 19
Last Quarter ◑ 12:36 AM EDT
► Moon void-of-course begins 7:05 AM EDT
Moon enters Gemini ♊ 8:06 AM EDT

SATURDAY, AUGUST 20

SUNDAY, AUGUST 21
► Moon void-of-course begins 6:06 PM EDT
Moon enters Cancer ♋ 8:29 PM EDT

Pomegranate

Apple

Fig

Basil

Homemade Bread -- Gratitude for Life

AUGUST 2022

Summer Harvest

MONDAY, AUGUST 22
⊙ Sun enters Virgo ♍ 11:16 PM EDT

Nasturtium

TUESDAY, AUGUST 23

Dill

WEDNESDAY, AUGUST 24
► Moon void-of-course begins 5:40 AM EDT
Moon enters Leo ♌ 9:07 AM EDT
♅℞ Uranus Retrograde 9:53 AM EDT - Jan. 22nd 2023

Celebrate with bread, herbed butter or oil, fruits, veggies, and edible flowers

THURSDAY, AUGUST 25

Vinegar

FRIDAY, AUGUST 26
► Moon void-of-course begins 2:55 AM EDT
Moon enters Virgo ♍ 8:24 PM EDT

SATURDAY, AUGUST 27
New Moon ● in Virgo ♍ 4:17 AM EDT

Anoint candles with olive oil and crushed basil

SUNDAY, AUGUST 28
► Moon void-of-course begins 11:08 PM EDT

Rye

Dianthus & Marigold

AUGUST/SEPTEMBER 2022

MONDAY, AUGUST 29
Moon enters Libra ♎ 5:25 AM EDT

TUESDAY, AUGUST 30

WEDNESDAY, AUGUST 31
► Moon void-of-course begins 6:43 AM EDT
Moon enters Scorpio ♏ 1:11 PM EDT

THURSDAY, SEPTEMBER 1

FRIDAY, SEPTEMBER 2
► Moon void-of-course begins 1:22 PM EDT
Moon enters Sagittarius ♐ 6:39 PM EDT

SATURDAY, SEPTEMBER 3
First Quarter ☽ 2:08 PM EDT

SUNDAY, SEPTEMBER 4
► Moon void-of-course begins 9:51 PM EDT
Moon enters Capricorn ♑ 10:02 PM EDT

Sculpt a crocodile out of clay and
emblazon it with jewels and crystals

SOBEK
EGYPTIAN GOD OF STRENGTH & PROTECTION

INTUITION | REFLECTION | INTENTIONS | IMPORTANT THINGS | GOALS

Virgo's Bag of Tricks
Tidiness
Practicality
The power of "everyday" magic and mundane tasks
POPPINS ALL-PURPOSE CLEANING
ALWAYS THROW SPILLED SALT OVER YOUR LEFT SHOULDER
MERCURY
The power of the mind
WITCH'S BOOK OF FACTS
Virtue
Work with sardonyx to attune to your values and integrity
Analysis
Enchant your notebook for mental prowess with a sprig of horehound or mint

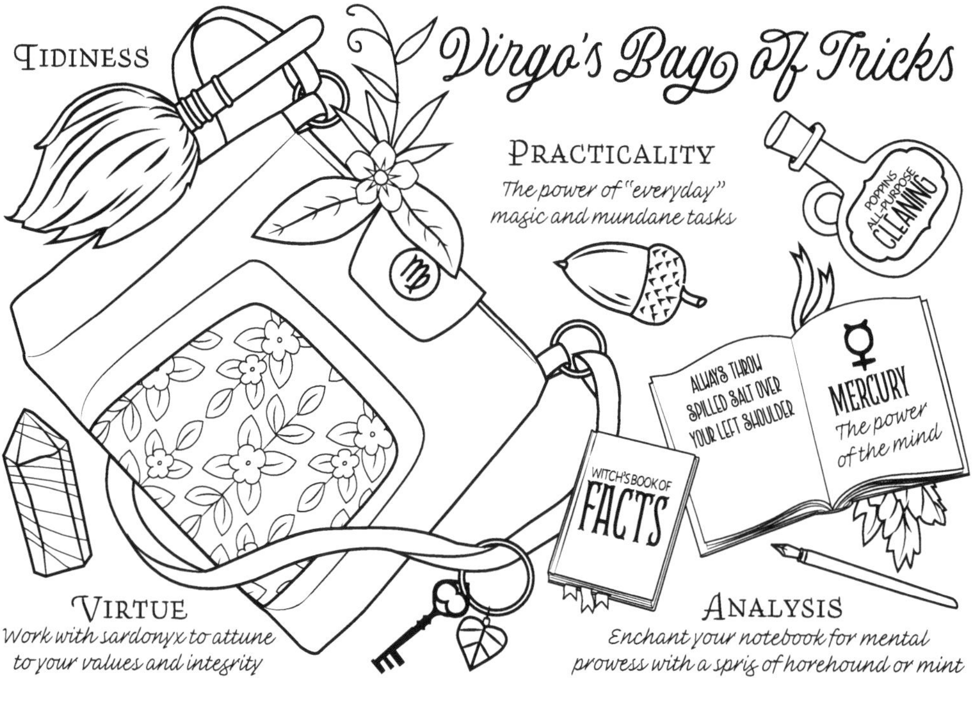

VIRGO

THE MAGIC OF PRACTICALITY

NEW & WAXING MOON: Analyze what needs to get done and plan the best way to do it
FULL MOON: Concentrate on your most important work or tasks that require a strong mind
WANING & DARK MOON: Clear out, release, banish, and get rid of what no longer serves you

Grow a wax plant near your magical tools to imbue them with extra power and protection

SEPTEMBER

GARLIC   Vinegar
BANISHING

ANISE   HYSSOP   MINT
PURIFICATION

GROUNDING

Pink Salt   RAINBOW PEPPERCORNS   Black Salt   Dead SEA Salt
PROTECTION

HAPPINESS

Protect your books and knowledge
with mugwort and sage sprigs

PRACTICAL MAGIC
A TIDY WITCH IS A POWERFUL WITCH

"All we are is dust in the wind." That may be true, but it won't stop a Virgo from sweeping up that dust and making some magic out of it.

Dust, dirt, and "earth" are essential parts of life. Virgo's superpower is all that is practical: dutifully combating the rougher edges of life and making order out of chaos.

A MAGICAL CLEANING RITUAL: Before you begin, put on your favorite music or audio. Set the sacred tone by diffusing essential oils, lighting candles, or simmering a pot of water mixed with aromatic herbs. And don't underestimate the power of a cleanliness. It will help you create space where mystical energy and inspiration flows.

SUMMON A GODDESS: Frau Holle is the Teutonic (German) deity of housework. Broom in hand, call her to give you strength to do the work.

BANISH THE MICROBES: If you want your witchy cleaning potions to "actually" clean, it's best to use things that have some antimicrobial properties. These essential oils will do the trick: lemon, clove, eucalyptus, oregano, rosemary, tea tree, thyme, peppermint, cedar, lavender, and lemongrass.

CLEANING POTIONS: Most witchy cleaning potions use about 13 ounces of water to 5 ounces of white vinegar mixed with 10 or 20 drops of essential oil. You can also boil herbs and water to make a decoction, then cool and strain.

SPRAYS AND ASPERGES: Asperges means to sprinkle water in a ritualistic manner. Pour your cleaning potion into a spray bottle or dip your mop, rag, or sprig of herbs into it to disperse where needed. As you clean, visualize the past and any worries sweeping away into oblivion.

MABON

CLEARING AND RELEASING
RITUALS TO TIDY UP THE ENERGY IN YOUR LIFE

Mabon, the Autumnal Equinox and seasonal shift from the light to dark, is a powerful time for clearing and releasing. You can smell it in the air—the fallen leaves and scent of the dirt, the trees, the rains, and the shift of the seasons.

While you can "clear the air" anytime, Mabon is auspicious. You might also consider this ritual if you've had arguments or felt intense emotions, or if you feel stagnant or creatively blocked. It's also helpful if you feel lost, anxious, or at sunrise or sunset. And of course—when you've had guests, or if you've been suspiciously unlucky.

BROOM IN HAND: Traditional broom spells sweep just above the floor in a counterclockwise "banishing" motion. Start in the center of the room and spiral outwards. Finish at an open door with a symbolic sweep of all the unwanted energy.

HERBS, SMOKE, & POTIONS: Burn herbs as cleansing incense, diffuse them as essential oils, or mix them up into spritzes and waters as in the previous spell. Use whatever herbs you prefer—however, here are some ideas.

CHILL OUT: Make a mix of vetivert, chamomile, and skullcap, and use as incense or tea.

HEAVY-DUTY: Burn a mix of basil, rue, rosemary, frankincense, and yarrow to clear the thickest air.

IN THE KITCHEN: Make your favorite recipe with chopped onions, garlic, and peppers.

CRYSTALS: Place crystals at the four corners of the house to absorb negative energy. Selenite is lovely for this. However you may prefer black tourmaline, obsidian, kyanite, or plain salt.

SOUND: Ring bells, play music, beat drums, and make all sorts of noise to shake up the energy.

SEPTEMBER 2022

	SUNDAY	MONDAY	TUESDAY
	28	29	30
	4	5	6
	11	12	13
	18	19	20
	25 New Moon ● ♎︎	26	27

WEDNESDAY	THURSDAY	FRIDAY	SATURDAY
31	1	2	3 First Quarter ◑
7	8	9 Mercury Retrograde Begins (Ends Oct. 2nd)	10 Full Moon ○ ✕
14	15	16	17 Last Quarter ◐
21	22 ☉ Sun enters Libra ✴ Mabon (Autumnal Equinox)	23	24
28	29	30	1

PRACTICALLY PERFECT
Black Tea + Rose Hips

SEPTEMBER 2022

MONDAY, SEPTEMBER 5

TUESDAY, SEPTEMBER 6
▸ Moon void-of-course begins 5:43 PM EDT
Moon enters Aquarius ♒ 11:41 PM EDT

WEDNESDAY, SEPTEMBER 7

THURSDAY, SEPTEMBER 8
▸ Moon void-of-course begins 8:34 AM EDT

FRIDAY, SEPTEMBER 9
Moon enters Pisces ♓ 12:44 AM EDT
☿℞ Mercury Retrograde 11:38 PM EDT - Oct. 2nd

SATURDAY, SEPTEMBER 10
Full Moon ○ in Pisces ♓ 5:59 AM EDT
▸ Moon void-of-course begins 8:29 PM EDT

SUNDAY, SEPTEMBER 11
Moon enters Aries ♈ 2:47 AM EDT

Elderflower

*Wisely using what
the Earth has given*

Virgo & Mercury
PRACTICAL MAGIC

SEPTEMBER 2022

MONDAY, SEPTEMBER 12

TUESDAY, SEPTEMBER 13
▶ Moon void-of-course begins 12:53 AM EDT
Moon enters Taurus ♉ 7:39 AM EDT

WEDNESDAY, SEPTEMBER 14

THURSDAY, SEPTEMBER 15
▶ Moon void-of-course begins 8:59 AM EDT
Moon enters Gemini ♊ 4:16 PM EDT

FRIDAY, SEPTEMBER 16

SATURDAY, SEPTEMBER 17
▶ Moon void-of-course begins 5:52 PM EDT
Last Quarter ☽ 5:52 PM EDT

SUNDAY, SEPTEMBER 18
Moon enters Cancer ♋ 4:00 AM EDT

APATITE
How can I increase my powers of practicality and service to others?

MOSS AGATE
How can I enjoy and feel gratitude for what I already have?

Valerian

SARDONYX
How can I process the information around me and use it as wisdom?

SEPTEMBER 2022

MONDAY, SEPTEMBER 19

TUESDAY, SEPTEMBER 20
► Moon void-of-course begins 11:57 AM EDT
Moon enters Leo ♌ 4:37 PM EDT

WEDNESDAY, SEPTEMBER 21

THURSDAY, SEPTEMBER 22
► Moon void-of-course begins 7:07 AM EDT
☉ Sun enters Libra ♎ 9:04 PM EDT
★ Mabon (Autumnal Equinox) 9:04 PM EDT

FRIDAY, SEPTEMBER 23
Moon enters Virgo ♍ 3:53 AM EDT

SATURDAY, SEPTEMBER 24

SUNDAY, SEPTEMBER 25
► Moon void-of-course begins 8:49 AM EDT
Moon enters Libra ♎ 12:43 PM EDT
New Moon ● in Libra ♎ 5:54 PM EDT

AIR WITCHERY
- Go outside on a windy day and listen to the wind and birds.
- Meditate facing east and imagine floating on a cloud of knowledge.
- Repeat a mantra like, "I always figure it out."
- Practice breathing exercises and things like chanting and singing.
- Run, walk, or otherwise feel the movement of your breath or body.

Parsley

Aspen

Mint

SEPTEMBER/OCTOBER 2022

MONDAY, SEPTEMBER 26

TUESDAY, SEPTEMBER 27
► Moon void-of-course begins 12:21 PM EDT
Moon enters Scorpio ♏ 7:14 PM EDT

WEDNESDAY, SEPTEMBER 28

THURSDAY, SEPTEMBER 29
► Moon void-of-course begins 5:20 PM EDT

FRIDAY, SEPTEMBER 30
Moon enters Sagittarius ♐ 12:02 AM EDT

SATURDAY, OCTOBER 1
► Moon void-of-course begins 5:46 PM EDT

SUNDAY, OCTOBER 2
☿℞ Mercury Retrograde ends 5:07 AM
Moon enters Capricorn ♑ 3:38 PM EDT
First Quarter ◐ 8:14 PM EDT

AIR
THE ELEMENT OF IDEAS

Libra's Bag Of Tricks

BEAUTY
Wash your face with rosewater before bed for beauty & prophetic dreams

HARMONY
Work with ametrine to harmonize two different energies or personalities

VENUS
Place rose quartz under your pillow when Venus is in Libra to make life more beautiful

LOVE
Carry pink tourmaline to attract love. Scatter hydrangea bark to repel it

Roses
- Love -

Venus - Cardinal - Air

"I Relate"

Grains &
Stonefruits

The Abundance
of Nature

LIBRA

THE MAGIC OF BALANCE

NEW & WAXING MOON: Shift your energy towards an area of life that needs more attention
FULL MOON: Plan a celebratory ritual that is socially gratifying and pleasing to the eye
WANING & DARK MOON: Spend time doing art or things that beautify your life and space

Blue Tourmaline
Harmony & Understanding

Morganite - Love & Enjoyment of Life

OCTOBER

THE SACRED BALANCE
SIMPLE SPELLCRAFT TO HARMONIZE YOUR LIFE

Libra is about a balance of things. A little of this, a little of that—listening to the wind and working to get the mix of elements just right.

Balance is critical for successful magic. If you swing too far one way, you are likely to veer off-course from center or lose control. The more balanced you can stay in body, mind, and spirit (and in your relationships and energetic exchanges), the better your magic (and life) will be.

This is also an excellent spell or ritual craft for Mabon (in September)—as the day and night are equal and the sun in Libra has just begun.

THE ENERGY: Have you been spending more love and care on others than on yourself, or vice versa? Or more time at work and not enough time for play or rest? Too much time analyzing and not enough dreaming, or the other way around? Use

tarot cards or introspection to figure out where you need to shift the load.

ON YOUR ALTAR: Create a symbol of balance. Procure a small vintage scale or make your own out of wire and a couple of ceramic dishes.

Or simply make two "piles" of representative objects that are symbolically equal.

MAKE A MOBILE: Find an attractive stick of your favorite wand wood, then hang and balance symbolic trinkets. Shells, beads, feathers, tiny crystals, found bones... you'll need to use your witchy senses to get it just right.

As you hang items on your mobile or place things on your altar scale, call out the intention of what you will shift and how. Use the energy of the season to let go, release, or "say no" to activities and things that have caused the imbalance.

Drink black currant and burdock tea to heighten the dark-side of your creativity

Mix a bit of ash or graveyard dirt into your paint to enchant it with the power of darkness

SAMHAIN

RITUAL MASKS
THE WITCH'S POWER OF BECOMING

Spiritual folk have worn masks in rituals and magical rites for thousands of years. There's a deep significance and a palpable change that occurs when you put on a mask or costume. You feel yourself become someone else, and with that, a door to spiritual and personal evolution opens.

There is so much power in masks, that costuming yourself as a wild creature would get you 3 years' imprisonment in Canterbury in the 7th century.

And if you're not the mask type, you can make a crown, hat, robe, or headdress.

Make a mask to represent your shadow and another to represent your light. Decorate accordingly, then wear them or use them as altar decorations.

Design a divination mask or veil. Enchant it with a sprig of eucalyptus, mugwort, or lilac for spiritual protection as you gaze into the mysteries beyond.

Craft a mask to channel your ancestors. Waft it through the smoke of myrrh or with water and anisette to enhance your spiritual connection.

Make a mask to see into your future or through the eyes of future generations. Consecrate it with herbs like mugwort and wormwood to induce visions and psychic powers.

Wear a mask that represents an animal or elemental spirit guide. Decorate it with natural treasures like shells, herbs, and magical woods.

Craft a mask to channel a deity or multiple deities such as the triple goddess—Maiden, Mother, and Crone. Research and adorn it with herbs, scents, and items that are specific to the presence you wish to channel.

Make a "classic" scary mask or hooded robe to frighten off whatever you wish to banish.

OCTOBER 2022

	SUNDAY	MONDAY	TUESDAY
	25 New Moon ● ♎︎ Mercury Retrograde Ends	26	27
	2 First Quarter ◑	3	4
	9 Full Moon ○ ♈︎	10	11
	16	17 Last Quarter ◑	18 Partial Solar Eclipse ♏︎ 7:01 AM EDT
	23 Saturn Retrograde Ends ☉ Sun enters Scorpio ♏︎	24	25 New Moon ● ♏︎
	30 Mars Retrograde Begins (Ends Jan. 12th 2023)	31 ★ Samhain (Fixed Date)	1 First Quarter ◑

WEDNESDAY	THURSDAY	FRIDAY	SATURDAY
28	29	30	1
5	6	7	8 *Pluto Retrograde Ends*
12	13	14	15
19	20	21	22
26	27	28	29
2	3	4	5

OCTOBER 2022

MONDAY, OCTOBER 3
▸ Moon void-of-course begins 11:49 PM EDT

TUESDAY, OCTOBER 4
Moon enters Aquarius ≈ 6:20 AM EDT

WEDNESDAY, OCTOBER 5
▸ Moon void-of-course begins 6:45 PM EDT

THURSDAY, OCTOBER 6
Moon enters Pisces ⓧ 8:48 AM EDT

FRIDAY, OCTOBER 7

SATURDAY, OCTOBER 8
▸ Moon void-of-course begins 7:10 AM EDT
Moon enters Aries ♈ 11:59 AM EDT
♇℞ Pluto Retrograde ends 5:55 PM EDT

SUNDAY, OCTOBER 9
Full Moon ◯ in Aries ♈ 4:55 PM EDT

Mint
Love & Luck

Jade

Harmony

Berries
Sweet Pleasures
of Life

Libra & Venus
BEAUTY & LOVE
If you see Venus in the morning, wish from
your heart. If you see her in the evening, spin
around six times and release your worries.

OCTOBER 2022

MONDAY, OCTOBER 10
► Moon void-of-course begins 10:02 AM EDT
Moon enters Taurus ♉ 5:05 PM EDT

TUESDAY, OCTOBER 11

WEDNESDAY, OCTOBER 12
► Moon void-of-course begins 5:42 PM EDT

THURSDAY, OCTOBER 13
Moon enters Gemini ♊ 1:10 AM EDT

FRIDAY, OCTOBER 14

SATURDAY, OCTOBER 15
► Moon void-of-course begins 12:11 AM EDT
Moon enters Cancer ♋ 12:12 PM EDT

SUNDAY, OCTOBER 16

SWORDS
Where can I make
a final decision?

LIZARDS
How can I walk
between worlds?

SAPPHIRE
Where is the center
of my being?

OCTOBER 2022

MONDAY, OCTOBER 17
Last Quarter ◖ 1:15 PM EDT
▸ Moon void-of-course begins 4:56 PM EDT

TUESDAY, OCTOBER 18
Moon enters Leo ♌ 12:44 AM EDT

WEDNESDAY, OCTOBER 19

THURSDAY, OCTOBER 20
▸ Moon void-of-course begins 6:35 AM EDT
Moon enters Virgo ♍ 12:22 PM EDT

FRIDAY, OCTOBER 21

SATURDAY, OCTOBER 22
▸ Moon void-of-course begins 2:17 PM EDT
Moon enters Libra ♎ 9:23 PM EDT

SUNDAY, OCTOBER 23
♄℞ Saturn Retrograde ends 12:07 AM EDT
☉ Sun enters Scorpio ♏ 6:35 AM EDT

*Anoint your Jack-O'-Lantern candle
with clove oil and a bit of cinnamon
for powerful protective magic*

OCTOBER 2022

MONDAY, OCTOBER 24
▶ Moon void-of-course begins 8:36 PM EDT

TUESDAY, OCTOBER 25
Moon enters Scorpio ♏ 3:15 AM EDT
New Moon ● in Scorpio ♏ 6:49 AM EDT
Partial Solar Eclipse in Scorpio ♏ 7:01 AM

WEDNESDAY, OCTOBER 26

THURSDAY, OCTOBER 27
▶ Moon void-of-course begins 12:27 AM EDT
Moon enters Sagittarius ♐ 6:55 AM EDT

FRIDAY, OCTOBER 28

SATURDAY, OCTOBER 29
▶ Moon void-of-course begins 9:10 AM EDT
Moon enters Capricorn ♑ 9:21 AM EDT

SUNDAY, OCTOBER 30
♂℞ Mars Retrograde 9:26 AM EDT - Jan. 12th 2023

Samhain Herbs

Star Anise
Spiritual & Ancestral
Connection

Vetivert Root
Protection &
Attraction

Agrimony
Protection &
Witch Power

Salt
Protection
& Purification

Licorice Root
Attraction

Mullein
Calling Ancestors
& Spirit Work

OCTOBER/NOVEMBER 2022

MONDAY, OCTOBER 31

★ Samhain (Fixed Festival Date)

▸ Moon void-of-course begins 11:14 AM EDT

Moon enters Aquarius ♒ 11:44 AM EDT

TUESDAY, NOVEMBER 1

First Quarter ◐ 2:37 AM EDT

WEDNESDAY, NOVEMBER 2

▸ Moon void-of-course begins 7:08 AM EDT

Moon enters Pisces ♓ 2:48 PM EDT

THURSDAY, NOVEMBER 3

FRIDAY, NOVEMBER 4

▸ Moon void-of-course begins 6:05 PM EDT

Moon enters Aries ♈ 7:07 PM EDT

SATURDAY, NOVEMBER 5

SUNDAY, NOVEMBER 6

▸ Moon void-of-course begins 6:30 PM EST

Anoint black candles with dark oils like vetivert, patchouli, and cloves. Burn them for protection.

Place a jar of water on a grave under the full moon. Remove it before dawn and use it for seances and spirit work.

Scorpio's Bag of Tricks

BRILLIANT
Carry a fluorite ball to connect to
the power of your higher intellect

STRANGE
Feel gratitude for the
things that make you unique

PLUTO
Ask for strength to face the
darkness when you see moths,
spiders, bats, or scorpions

ENERGETIC
Charge your aura with rhododendrons
and other bright red flowers

UNUSUAL
Do something at night that you
would normally do in the day

Scorpion
The Power of
Transformation

Pluto - Fixed - Water - "I Can"

Witch Hazel
makes a lovely
divining rod

Azalea
Feminine Power

Hawthorn

Blackthorn

MEMENTO MORI

SCORPIO

THE MAGIC OF TRANSFORMATION

NEW & WAXING MOON: Think of ways you wish to transform or step into the unknown
FULL MOON: Channel all of your power and will towards the deepest desire of your soul
WANING & DARK MOON: Sit in a dark bath surrounded by crystals and regain your power

Venus Fly Trap
Attraction & Protection

POWER

Passion

WEALTH

Burn crushed willow bark and sandalwood at the
waning or dark moon to connect to your spirit

NOVEMBER

WATERS DARK AND DEEP
RITUAL BATHS OF TRANSFORMATION

What lies beneath the surface of your conscious mind? Something powerful and weirdly specific to you, no doubt. You might stuff all sorts of things into that dark well—mysteries, lost agendas, things left unsaid, and un-lived experiences that your soul so deeply wishes to have. *Le sigh!* And dredging up these shadows is essential to living a magical life.

Scorpio has a powerful sting, and a hidden depth of esoteric wisdom. The emotions that wake you in the night—life, death, sex, power, loss, redemption—these are the notes of Scorpio's song.

There is nothing gentle about Scorpio. It isn't a healing water, but a volatile and transformational one. It is the ocean changing the shape of the shoreline, a river cutting through rock.

DARK AQUATIC RITUALS AND MOON BATHS: Perform these rituals in a body of water—a pool, tub, lake, ocean, stream—or just envision them in the waters of your mind's eye. You can also prepare some water and herbs in a bowl and pour them over your head in the shower.

DARK MOON THEME to release things: prepare a bath with sea salts and kava-kava root. Submerge yourself in the water. When you emerge, you will leave behind what you wish to release.

FULL MOON THEME to gather energy or wisdom, or to transform: prepare a bath with damiana, ginger, and ylang-ylang oil or another sultry scent. Submerge yourself underwater and ask for guidance. When you emerge, you will receive an answer or find the solution shortly thereafter.

To transform, envision yourself how you wish to be while submerged under water. When you emerge from the water, you have become it.

NOVEMBER 2022

	SUNDAY	MONDAY	TUESDAY
	Mars Retrograde Begins (Ends Jan. 12th 2023) 30	★ Samhain (Fixed Date) 31	1 First Quarter ◐
	6	★ Samhain 5:36 AM EST 7	Total Lunar Eclipse ♉ 5:59 AM EST 8 Full Moon ○ ♉
	13	14	15
	20	21	⊙ Sun Enters Sagittarius 22
	27	28	29

WEDNESDAY	THURSDAY	FRIDAY	SATURDAY
2	3	4	5
9	10	11	12
16 Last Quarter ◐ *Jupiter Retrograde Ends*	17	18	19
23 New Moon ●♐	24	25	26 *Neptune Retrograde Ends*
30 First Quarter ◑	1	2	3

NOVEMBER 2022

MONDAY, NOVEMBER 7
Moon enters Taurus ♉ 12:17 AM EST
★ Samhain (Astronomical Date) 5:36 AM EST

TUESDAY, NOVEMBER 8
Total Lunar Eclipse in Taurus ♉ 5:59 AM
Full Moon ○ in Taurus ♉ 6:02 AM EST

WEDNESDAY, NOVEMBER 9
▸ Moon void-of-course begins 7:00 AM EST
Moon enters Gemini ♊ 8:37 AM EST

THURSDAY, NOVEMBER 10

FRIDAY, NOVEMBER 11
▸ Moon void-of-course begins 5:28 PM EST
Moon enters Cancer ♋ 7:22 PM EST

SATURDAY, NOVEMBER 12

SUNDAY, NOVEMBER 13

Datura
Power of the Darkness

Scorpio & Pluto
ESOTERIC ENERGY
*Gaze into the black of night with
your eyes open and ask questions*

NOVEMBER 2022

MONDAY, NOVEMBER 14
▸ Moon void-of-course begins 5:41 AM EDT
Moon enters Leo ♌ 7:47 AM EST

TUESDAY, NOVEMBER 15

WEDNESDAY, NOVEMBER 16
Last Quarter ☽ 8:27 AM EST
▸ Moon void-of-course begins 6:55 PM EST
Moon enters Virgo ♍ 8:03 PM EST

THURSDAY, NOVEMBER 17

FRIDAY, NOVEMBER 18

SATURDAY, NOVEMBER 19
▸ Moon void-of-course begins 3:46 AM EST
Moon enters Libra ♎ 5:58 AM EST

SUNDAY, NOVEMBER 20

OPAL
What intuitive messages have I been unwilling to accept?

Honeysuckle
How can I trust the power and strength of my intuition?

SPIDER
How can I weave the impossible?

NOVEMBER 2022

MONDAY, NOVEMBER 21
► Moon void-of-course begins 6:14 AM EST
Moon enters Scorpio ♏ 12:16 PM EST

TUESDAY, NOVEMBER 22
☉ Sun enters Sagittarius ♐ 3:20 AM EST

WEDNESDAY, NOVEMBER 23
► Moon void-of-course begins 1:16 PM EST
Moon enters Sagittarius ♐ 3:14 PM EST
New Moon ● in Sagittarius ♐ 5:57 PM EST
♃℞ Jupiter Retrograde ends 6:02 PM EST

THURSDAY, NOVEMBER 24

FRIDAY, NOVEMBER 25
► Moon void-of-course begins 2:22 PM EST
Moon enters Capricorn ♑ 4:18 PM EST

SATURDAY, NOVEMBER 26

SUNDAY, NOVEMBER 27
► Moon void-of-course begins 3:11 PM EST
Moon enters Aquarius ♒ 5:07 PM EST

SPIRIT
THE ELEMENT OF CONSCIOUSNESS

NOVEMBER/DECEMBER 2022

MONDAY, NOVEMBER 28

TUESDAY, NOVEMBER 29
► Moon void-of-course begins 1:53 AM EST
Moon enters Pisces ♓ 7:15 PM EST

WEDNESDAY, NOVEMBER 30
First Quarter ◑ 9:36 AM EST

THURSDAY, DECEMBER 1
► Moon void-of-course begins 9:44 PM EST
Moon enters Aries ♈ 11:43 PM EST

FRIDAY, DECEMBER 2

SATURDAY, DECEMBER 3
♆℞ Neptune Retrograde ends 7:15 PM

SUNDAY, DECEMBER 4
► Moon void-of-course begins 12:46 AM EST
Moon enters Taurus ♉ 6:38 AM EST

HEDGE WITCHERY

- Feel the spirit of all things.
- Seek out relationships with your spirit guides.
- Look for the meanings and lessons in everything.
- Make your own way in life and always follow your spirit first.
- Go as far as you can into the power of your mind and meditations.
- Delve deep into shadow work.

Burn sandalwood to connect to spirit

Apophyllite Pyramid Opening the Third Eye

Sagittarius's Bag of Tricks

HONESTY

Work with jasper to be honest about
which direction you want to go in life

INTELLECT

Place a sprig of sage in
your pocket or book to
gain wisdom

JUPITER

Place star anise at the four
corners to expand the energy
of your magic circle

INDEPENDENCE

Wear a horse charm or dandelion
crown to free your spirit

The Archer
Shooting for the Stars

Jupiter - Mutable - Fire - "I Understand"

Golden Topaz
your Highest Self

SAGITTARIUS

THE MAGIC OF PERSONAL GROWTH

NEW & WAXING MOON: Explore new ideas, topics, and adventures that you want to pursue
FULL MOON: Gather power and launch yourself in the direction your heart wants you to go
WANING & DARK MOON: Take time to try new foods, read, daydream, and wander aimlessly

Licorice

Mint

Anise

Bay

Black Currants

DECEMBER

Rosemary

Parsley

Onions & Garlic

HEARTH AND SPICE
KITCHEN WITCHERY TO STOKE YOUR FLAME

The hearth is a symbol of ancestry and the cycle of birth, life, and death.

If your hearth fire went out in ancient Celtic times, misfortune would befall you, so people went to great lengths to keep hearth fires stoked.

Sagittarius embodies the energy of a kitchen fire or hearth deity—the scent of spices, a radiant heat, and an enticing aura of danger that may burst into magical flames at any moment.

In this spell, you'll use the power of spice and light to refresh the energy of your hearth, the undying light of life within your home.

PREPARE by focusing on the things that give light and heat in your kitchen. Clean them all thoroughly. The spice rack, oven, windows, and light fixtures to name a few—hard work, but doing so will yield magical results.

Purchase at least one new spice or refill an old favorite. If you're up to it, create, reorganize, redecorate, or replenish your entire spice cabinet.

Craft an altar in your kitchen, perhaps a clay dish with candles and symbols of deities, fire, and light. Or gather a collection of potent herbs and spices like peppers, onions, garlic, and basil.

RAISE ENERGY: Anoint a spell candle with kitchen magic—roll it in olive oil, then in crushed spices such as cinnamon, rosemary, and thyme.

Light the spell candle at your kitchen altar. Hold your hands to the warmth of the flame while you dedicate yourself to stoking the flames of life within yourself and home.

Commit to "stoking the hearth fire" as a daily ritual either with candles or by eating something with spice and feeling the energy of life within.

Make an embroidered
lucky poppet stuffed
with moss & herbs

YULE

Pink Topaz
Hope & Divinity

THE SPIRIT OF GIVING
A SPELL TO SHARE MAGIC AND WARMTH

The festivals and traditions of the winter solstice, the darkest day of the year, have merged from many ancient cultures (a phenomenon called syncretism) into modern Christmas and neo-pagan Yule.

The practice of giving gifts began as early as the Roman festival of Saturnalia. Ancient people gave in honor of Saturn, the god of agriculture and time, as the sun moves back into Capricorn (ruled by Saturn) on the winter solstice.

Saturnalia gifts were often practical, although outrageous, opulent, or comical items were not uncommon. It was also traditional to write a short, personalized poem with each gift.

TAPERED CANDLES are symbolic gestures of the sun's light. Anoint gift candles with amber oil to signify the sun or cypress for the power of Saturn.

SPOONS & CUPS: Housewares have made nice prezzies for thousands of years. Give ceremonial spoons with painted or wood-burned sigils, or earthy clay cups, bowls, and incense burners.

FOOD: Give a taste of ancient Saturnalia with herbal vinegar, oil, spiced wine, cakes, and cookies.

DOLLS & POPPETS: Make dolls for play or dedicate them to deities or magical workings. Stuff them with symbolic dried herbs and mosses.

STATIONERY and writing implements are just as handy now as they were in 130 BC. Add a drop of perfumed oil or crushed herbs for a magical aura.

A RITUAL OF GIVING: At dawn, pile up the gifts you are giving in the center of the room. Circle around the gifts clockwise, three times, imagining a bright light swirling around. Ring bells, sing, and otherwise release as much good cheer as you can into the gifts and to the world.

Create a powerful beverage with mulled spice. Heat your favorite dark fruity tea with apple cider, honey, orange slices, and spices like nutmeg, cinnamon, star anise, cardamom, and cloves.

DECEMBER 2022

SUNDAY	MONDAY	TUESDAY
27	28	29
4	5	6
11	12	13
18	19	20
25	26	27

WEDNESDAY	THURSDAY	FRIDAY	SATURDAY
			Neptune Retrograde Ends
30 First Quarter	1	2	3
7 Full Moon ○ ♊	8	9	10
14	15	16 Last Quarter ◑	17
★ Yule (Winter Solstice) ☉ Sun enters Capricorn 21	22	23 New Moon ● ♑	24
28	Mercury Retrograde Begins (Ends Jan. 18th 2023) 29 First Quarter ◐	30	31

DECEMBER 2022

MONDAY, DECEMBER 5

TUESDAY, DECEMBER 6
▸ Moon void-of-course begins 2:02 PM EST
Moon enters Gemini ♊ 3:50 PM EST

WEDNESDAY, DECEMBER 7
Full Moon ○ in Gemini ♊ 11:08 PM EST

THURSDAY, DECEMBER 8

FRIDAY, DECEMBER 9
▸ Moon void-of-course begins 1:13 AM EST
Moon enters Cancer ♋ 2:50 AM EST

SATURDAY, DECEMBER 10

SUNDAY, DECEMBER 11
▸ Moon void-of-course begins 1:49 PM EST
Moon enters Leo ♌ 3:09 PM EST

Ash

Oak
Power & Protection

Birch

Sagittarius & Jupiter
The Archer
Find Jupiter in the sky. Think about where
you are and how far you want to go.

DECEMBER 2022

MONDAY, DECEMBER 12

TUESDAY, DECEMBER 13
▸ Moon void-of-course begins 10:52 AM EST

WEDNESDAY, DECEMBER 14
Moon enters Virgo ♍ 3:43 AM EST

THURSDAY, DECEMBER 15

FRIDAY, DECEMBER 16
Last Quarter ◑ 3:56 AM EST
▸ Moon void-of-course begins 2:13 PM EST
Moon enters Libra ♎ 2:47 PM EST

SATURDAY, DECEMBER 17

SUNDAY, DECEMBER 18
▸ Moon void-of-course begins 5:35 PM EST
Moon enters Scorpio ♏ 10:31 PM EST

CARNATION
How can I trust and strengthen my psychic powers?

DEER
How can I free the true essence of my spirit?

DANDELION
What is the most sincere wish of my heart?

DECEMBER 2022

MONDAY, DECEMBER 19

TUESDAY, DECEMBER 20
▸ Moon void-of-course begins 9:45 PM EST

WEDNESDAY, DECEMBER 21
Moon enters Sagittarius ♐ 2:13 AM EST
★ Yule (Winter Solstice) 4:48 PM EST
☉ Sun enters Capricorn ♑ 4:48 PM EST

THURSDAY, DECEMBER 22
▸ Moon void-of-course begins 3:16 PM EST

FRIDAY, DECEMBER 23
Moon enters Capricorn ♑ 2:47 AM EST
New Moon ● in Capricorn ♑ 5:17 AM EST

SATURDAY, DECEMBER 24
▸ Moon void-of-course begins 10:11 PM EST

SUNDAY, DECEMBER 25
Moon enters Aquarius ♒ 2:15 AM EST

- Poinsettia -
Festivity & Generosity

Evergreens
Resurrection & Immortality

DECEMBER 2022

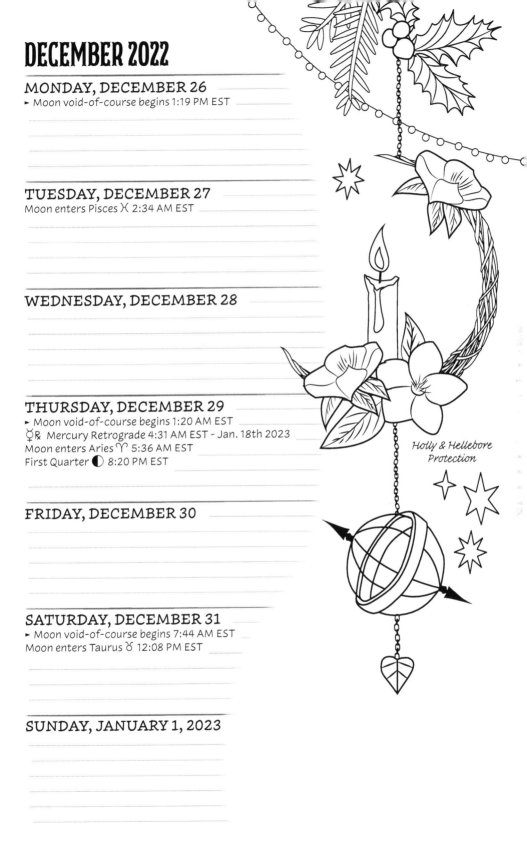

MONDAY, DECEMBER 26
➤ Moon void-of-course begins 1:19 PM EST

TUESDAY, DECEMBER 27
Moon enters Pisces ♓ 2:34 AM EST

WEDNESDAY, DECEMBER 28

THURSDAY, DECEMBER 29
➤ Moon void-of-course begins 1:20 AM EST
☿℞ Mercury Retrograde 4:31 AM EST - Jan. 18th 2023
Moon enters Aries ♈ 5:36 AM EST
First Quarter ◐ 8:20 PM EST

FRIDAY, DECEMBER 30

SATURDAY, DECEMBER 31
➤ Moon void-of-course begins 7:44 AM EST
Moon enters Taurus ♉ 12:08 PM EST

SUNDAY, JANUARY 1, 2023

Holly & Hellebore
Protection

Dance wildly or scream in your fiercest yell to channel Kali Ma

Burn something significant from this year to symbolize transition & transformation

KALI MA

HINDU GODDESS OF TIME & EVOLUTION

SUCCESS
What was my
biggest success?

RELEASE
What is best
left behind?

RECEIVE
What was 2022's
unexpected gift?

LESSONS
What've I learned
or overcome
this year?

GRATITUDE
What am I
most grateful for
in this past year?

Pull tarot cards, cast rune stones, or write
your own words of wisdom of what's passed
and the possibilities of what's to come.

Reflecting Back on 2022...

FOCUS
Where should my
energy go as the
year begins?

WISDOM
What wisdom will
guide me forward
in the best way
possible?

CHALLENGE
What challenge
lies ahead?

OPPORTUNITY
Where does my
greatest opportunity lie?

MAGIC
What new skills,
powers, or magic
should I cultivate?

Moving Forward Into 2023...

BIBLIOGRAPHY
and special thanks

Wendy Ledger
Editor
WendyLedgerAuthor.com

Fiona Horne
Editor of Magick
& Editor
FionaHorne.com

Kae Marie Denino
Editor

TWELVE FACES OF THE GODDESS
DANIELLE BLACKWOOD

Grimoire For The Green Witch
ANNE MOURA

THE COFFEE TABLE BOOK
OF ASTROLOGY

WOMEN'S DICTIONARY
OF SYMBOLS
BARBARA WALKER

THE ONLY ASTROLOGY BOOK YOU'LL EVER NEED
JOANNA MARTINE WOOLFOLD

THE ASTROLOGICAL MOON
HAYDN PAUL

PLANETS AND POSSIBILITIES
SUSAN MILLER

CUNNINGHAM'S
ENCYCLOPEDIA OF MAGICAL HERBS

TASCHEN'S
ASTROLOGY

PARKER'S ASTROLOGY

MANSIONS OF THE MOON
ANN MOURA

ASTROLOGICAL TRANSITS
APRIL ELLIOTT KENT

DO YOU LIKE THIS BOOK?! LEAVE A REVIEW!

About the Artist

Amy Cesari
(and her familiar, Cornelius)

Amy is an author and illustrator who loves animated musicals. She also likes watercolor painting, witchcraft, and walking on the beach in a really big sun hat. Not only does she own every Nintendo game console ever made, she's earned several fancy diplomas and enjoys continued studies in various magical practices.

CONTACT AMY AND SEE MORE BOOKS, PRINTABLE PAGES, AND ART :

Amy@coloringbookofshadows.com
ColoringBookofShadows.com